The Squirrel Method

Find Your Nuts and Get Rich!

Dr. Stephanie Aldrich

Disclaimer

Although the author and publisher have made every effort to ensure that the information in this e-book was correct at press time, the author and publisher do not assume and hereby disclaim any liability to any party for any loss, damage, or disruption caused by errors or omissions, whether such errors or omissions result from negligence, accident, or any other cause.

This e-book is not intended as a substitute for the financial advice of professional financial brokers, planners, and insurance agents.

This e-book is not intended as a substitute for the medical, marital, or spiritual advice of physicians, psychologists, counselors, therapists, and clergymen. The reader should regularly consult these professionals in matters relating to their physical and mental health, particularly concerning any symptoms that may require diagnosis or medical attention.

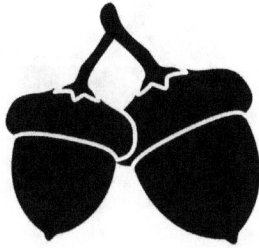

Dedication

To my son Noah and my future grandchildren:

If you follow *The Squirrel Method*, you too can live a rich life!

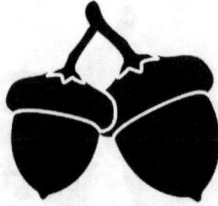

Table of Contents

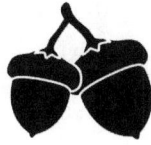

Acknowledgements

There are so many people who have been influential, instrumental, and inspirational to me during the creation of this book and I wanted to acknowledge some of them here.

My family, Debbie, Frank, and Heather who have taught me the importance of hard work and determination. Without your love and encouragement early in my life, I wouldn't be where I am today!

My grandparents, Roxanne, Richard, Frank, and Ann- who taught me how to live *The Squirrel Method*! You taught me the importance of money and how to live an abundant life doing what you love.

My husband Steven, my loving friend and partner who always supports my crazy ideas! I love ya!

My friend and financial advisor Amanda, thanks for helping me multiply my nuts and for giving me the idea for this book! Meeeeemeeeee!

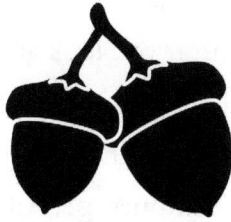

Introduction

I love analogies. Analogies help to explain how two different things are alike. "You're moving as slow as molasses" is an analogy. If you've ever poured molasses out of a jar, you will know that it's so thick and dense that it takes some time for it to move out of the jar on its own. If you're moving that slow, then you realize that you may want to stop the distractions and move it!

The purpose of this book is twofold:

1. To move you through the analogy that humans and squirrels are similar in their actions.

2. If you want to simplify your life and base your decisions on actions that will create success, then make the only decision that squirrels make every single day: to survive.

I know, it's a simple, watered-down statement on our life's purpose, but if you look at The Squirrel Methodology, you'll realize that all squirrels and the rest of the animal kingdom for that matter, are successful. All squirrels are living their purpose. All squirrels have rich lives. If they don't, they're dead, plain and simple. We humans can walk down the same road. Maybe we're not physically dead yet, but maybe we're stuck living a dead end life. Maybe we're unhappy. Maybe we're broke. Maybe we are sick and unhealthy. Isn't that a form of death?

Many philosophers would argue that in order to live a happy life, you've got to find your purpose. Without a purpose, you're aimlessly wandering the planet until you find death. That's where the squirrel analogy comes into play. As I've evolved in my middle-aged years, I've focused my resources on living my purpose. I've learned from successful and not-so- successful family and friends. The purpose of *The Squirrel Method* is to look at a simple creature like a squirrel and gather powerful similarities that can be tied to their successful survival and adapt those similarities to our lives.

My mother taught me to always have money available. She used the envelope system to save money for designated uses. For all of you Dave Ramsey followers out there, you know the envelope system of stashing cash in different envelopes so you could pay for school supplies, a vacation, or groceries. As activities came up that required financial obligations, my mom would store money in those designated envelopes so when the time came to pay the piper, she always had the cash available. Whether it was Christmas gifts or vacations, she always had the money. My paternal grandparents were the same way. They never kept their money in the same place and always worked to produce more. They then had the discipline to save most of it and multiply it through investments.

As I've grown older, I've developed my own survival system and have gathered all of the information that has made me a successful businesswoman so that I could pass it along to you. Don't take the theme of this book too lightly. The concepts it contains can help you change the areas in your life that need improving and allow you to not only survive, but thrive.

Living by *The Squirrel Method* is not just about finding your money nuts, although we talk in great detail about finances because a healthy financial life is very important to your freedom of choice for you and your family. Especially when you realize that 78% of Americans live paycheck to paycheck according to a 2019 Forbes article. Earning, keeping, and multiplying your money then becomes a very important subject. But it's not all about money. What about your health and energy? What about your time? What about your relationships, family, and friends? Living by *The Squirrel Method* encompasses all areas of life.

As you age and gain experience in life, you will soon realize that in order to live the way you want, you must *control* these areas of your life. You can't allow other people or activities to influence these areas. If you give up control, other people will use your resources for *their* own gains and you won't have anything left for yourself.

The Squirrel Method simplifies the way you think and approach life's big topics of resources, decision making, and mindset. If things become simple, you can easily and quickly become a master of those things. When things become complicated, progress never seems to be made.

The strategies and ideas that are conveyed in the *The Squirrel Method* are even more important during the post Covid times that we are living in right now. Now is the exact time that you should be working on not only your financial well-being, but also your physical, relational, and spiritual growth that can help you to live a long and prosperous life.

If anything, the Covid pandemic drew back the curtains in everyone's lives and showed them how truly strong or susceptible they were to their economy and their physical limitations. Many people, including myself, used the pandemic to draw the line in the sand and truly make big decisions and changes that affected everything in their lives. If there were any time to make sweeping life-altering changes for the better, it is now and The Squirrel Methodology can certainly put you and your family on the road to success.

Are you ready to simplify your life, find your nuts, and get rich?

Chapter 1

The Squirrel Method

I know the title of this book is cute and creative, but *The Squirrel Method* is not about stealing bird seed from some feeder or seeing how much food you can shove in your cheeks. Rather it's a life mantra that can be learned and utilized to live a prosperous life. People that take advantage of *The Squirrel Method* principles set themselves up to live an abundant and secure life.

One of my favorite quotes is by Benjamin Franklin that says, "You plan to fail if you fail to plan." This quote explains *The Squirrel Method* at its core. It has to do with planning and making sure that all the effort done today is focused on what it is you want to accomplish in the future. You can certainly manifest your future if you pay attention to what you're doing today!

Throughout this book, I will ask you questions that will make you start thinking about the present and what it is you want to achieve in the future. It's a simple method that anyone can use but don't take it too lightly, because your future depends on the seeds you plant today! You can use *The Squirrel Method* in any area of your life including financial, spiritual, emotional, and logical. It's completely universal.

What is your main purpose here on Earth? I don't need to get too deep here, but everyone has a different take on this common question and I want to make sure we're on the same wavelength before we move on. What is your main purpose? Is it to contribute? Is it to be prosperous and self-sufficient? Is it to create our own environment and economy? Is it to provide ourselves and those we love with the basic necessities? Is it to love? Is it to connect with God or whatever higher Spirit you believe in? Is it to gain knowledge?

If you answered "Yes" to any or all of these things, then you and I are in agreement with each other and on the same wavelength. I believe our purpose is all of these things I mentioned earlier. Let's break them down one by one and start thinking about how we're going to start applying *The Squirrel Method* to each.

Question #1: Is it to contribute?

The Squirrel Method: Squirrels help to clean up the environment. They not only eat the nuts off the trees, but they can also eat insects, fruit, flowers, plants, and veggies. The biggest way they contribute to the entire planet is they are natural farmers. They plant so many seeds and nuts over their lifetimes that naturally trees and plants begin to grow because of their abundant effort. They naturally replant our forests. That's a huge contribution to our planet, all from our cute furry friends.

How will *you* contribute? Everyone has some type of unique talent or ability. Some of us are very strong. Some of us are very intelligent. Others are very creative or good at problem-solving. Where do you fit in this spectrum of talented humans? What talents and abilities do you possess that can contribute to society? What's your purpose?

Most of us go to school, get training in some area that we like, and piddle through life allowing other people and other circumstances to control it. Why? Maybe because there's so many of us on this planet that we feel insignificant, like our efforts don't matter. In reality though, they are *very* important and even *crucial* to our civilization. What's that for being significant?

You are a creative and unique person! Many people in the spiritual community believe that we are spirits trapped in physical bodies trying to get out. Call it a soul. Call it heart. Call it your energy or inner voice. It doesn't matter what you call it, as long as you know it exists. How are you expressing that inner spirit? Are you listening to your inner voice when it tells you to go get that job, shoot that shot, take that trip, or talk to that person?

What is that inner voice telling you to do? We're not talking about schizophrenia here. We're talking about your spirit that's yearning to get out. To contribute and make a difference. How will you make a difference? This could be to invent a new product that could solve a problem that we have. This could be a service that could help others. This could be to donate time or energy in a charity event. This could also be to donate money towards a good cause. The ways of contributing are endless!

The question is, what are *you* doing? What contribution are you making to others? This question goes above and beyond your mundane routines that everyone gets into. This question goes much, much deeper than that. Most people never get that deep. Most people are only concerned with themselves and I get it. But what happens when you get all that you want? I'm not talking about just money here. What will you do when your basic needs are met, you have some surplus, and you get bored with your routines? Now we're getting somewhere! Now you're starting to really understand the question of contribution.

How will you make a difference?

Being human and living on this planet is truly an experience. We can feel the breeze through our hair. We can feel the water on our feet. We can smell the flowers in the summer. We can enjoy the changing seasons. Eat fresh fruit after the harvest and enjoy a bike ride through the park.

God has blessed us with so much. How will we give back? By contributing and helping others. By sharing our knowledge and unique talents and abilities with others. By expressing the need to make the human experience richer and authentic. All of this starts with you.

Even though you may feel overwhelmed or insignificant, it all starts with little old you. Each one of us has the obligation and duty to express ourselves and use our talents and abilities and contribute. No matter how big or small, we have a duty to contribute.

Question #2: Is it to be prosperous and self-sufficient?

The Squirrel Method: Squirrels are very independent creatures. They learn from other squirrels and from their mothers. Some types of squirrels live in packs while others are loners. Squirrels don't share. They gather enough food for themselves and make sure they stay busy enough to take care of themselves.

Humans aren't as independent as the squirrels. We rely heavily on others to provide convenience and our basic needs. Look at the Welfare statistics in this country. According to LexingtonLaw.com, in the U.S. 21% or 63 million Americans receive some type of government assistance. The Welfare system was started during the Great Depression in 1935 to help with the widespread poverty, starvation, and unemployment. Nowadays it consists of 79 different programs amounting to over $1 Trillion every year. Almost ½ of the people enrolled in housing and food stamps have been enrolled for over three years.

Are these people demonstrating squirrel methodology? Certainly not. Being self-sufficient doesn't mean using the resources of others as a main source of survival. Self-sufficiency means to be able to take care of your own basic necessities such as food, shelter, and clothing. In order to do this, you have to dig deep and bring your unique skills and talents to the surface. Not all of us can be entertainers, mechanics, teachers, or doctors. Those people are expressing their uniqueness to the world.

What most people lack is the persistence to contribute and bring those talents and abilities to the rest of us. Everyone has difficult times they go through. This is all part of the human experience. The ones who succeed get up, brush themselves off, and fight for another day. Those that give up, depend on others for survival.

The question you must ask yourself is, are you going to get back up and fight another day or are you going to give up and depend on others? This is a question that you'll have to answer for yourself. I know what my answer is, I want to continue to fight! I don't even like taking out loans from the banks anymore. It unnerves me that someone else has more resources than I do and I usually try to save as much money as I can to pay off my debt early. I want to live independently. I want to be financially free. I don't want to be bogged down by credit card debt or other bank loans.

According to Debt.org, Americans are over $13.5 Trillion in debt including mortgages, auto loans, credit cards, and student loans. That's a lot of debt! Most loans have interest rates of 5-7% APR so it's no wonder that if we want to live a comfortable life, that we have to depend on big banks to borrow money and find ourselves always underwater.

Being in debt or being on Welfare is not in accordance with The Squirrel Methodology. Being self-sufficient requires a lot of planning, sacrifice, and hard work to be independent from big banks and corporations who control a lot of things. How can we be more independent like the squirrels?

- We reap what we sow. We educate ourselves on skills that are in demand in the market and then we share those skills with them.

- We can budget our money and live within our means. I know, that's easier said than done, but it is very possible. Many younger people are opting out of purchasing homes and cars and leasing instead. Some are even paying for college as they go to avoid large debt amounts upon graduation.

· We can prioritize how we spend our money. Do we really *need* that pair of boots or do we *want* them? Needs versus wants can help you prioritize your budget and make it easier to decide how you spend your money.

· Figure out what the true cost of that item is if you borrow money to pay for it and how much you're paying in interest. The number may shock you and deter you from purchasing that item.

Those four concepts aren't easy, but they are necessary if you're going to live independently and be self-sufficient.

Question #3. Is it to create our own environment and economy?

The Squirrel Method: They don't ask permission from other squirrels to live in a certain tree or if that particular nut is theirs. They instinctively do these things. They take care of themselves. They create their own environment and their own stash of bounty.

Humans are different from squirrels in that we not only have instincts but we also have reasoning and logic. It's the reasoning and logic that can either provide us with a steady economy and safe environment, or not. We talked earlier about being self-sufficient and independent. What exactly does this mean? Being independent means that your survival depends on your own habitual behavior and ideas and not those of other people. The line that you must cross is if you believe that *you* can control your own destiny or if you are controlled by *it*. Those are two completely different ways of viewing the world and your role in it.

If you believe that you are controlled by your environment, by rules that were previously made, and you have to follow the path that you were born into. That way of thinking is completely different from someone who believes that there are endless possibilities and that they make their own path in life. One is independent and one is dependent.

This is a big question that you must answer for yourself if you want to live a prosperous and abundant life. For you to contribute your talents and abilities to the world, you must be able to create your own environment and economy. You must be able to take care of your basic needs and then have a *surplus* of resources to share with others. If you're depending on luck, circumstance, or someone else to create this for you, you're going to be waiting a long time!

No one that has ever made a contribution to society waited for someone else to lead the way. These people showed courage and kept their vision clear on what their contribution and purpose would become. They didn't allow their present circumstances to dictate their future outcomes. These pioneers used whatever they had currently, their ideas, their money, and their persistence to bring forth their unique talents and abilities. They were then rewarded monetarily, spiritually, and emotionally. How satisfied was Thomas Edison when the light bulb first was lit after failing over 10,000 times? How satisfied was Tim Berners-Lee who created the world wide web that we use to connect with other businesses and people from all around the world?

What if there was no Michael Jordan, Babe Ruth, or Muhammad Ali? Without an inner belief in their abilities and talents, milestones would never have been met or exceeded. What about Warren Buffett, Steve Jobs, or Bill Gates? Without their desire to solve problems and build wealth, this world we live in would be very different.

What about the first immigrants that came to the U.S? If they didn't believe that they could take care of themselves and contribute to their community, we wouldn't even be here. The Crusaders. The early artists. The explorers and pioneers. Without their willingness to create an environment they *wanted* to live in, rather than *forced* to live in, we wouldn't have the freedom and liberties that we enjoy today.

The problem with today's society is that we stand on a huge foundation built by these awe-inspiring people. Most major struggles have been dealt with and overcome. We have created the science and technology to make our lives comfortable and easily managed. But is this it? Is this all that our environment can be? Will we always have class disparities, sickness, and depression? Will there be no more pioneers born today that will create their own environment and toot their own horns? I definitely hope not! I want people to express their uniqueness so that everyone can benefit from it. I want us to improve our technology and cure cancer, visit new planets, and end poverty.

Humans are unique in that we can use our mental faculties to create anything we want. But we must be willing to create it and not sit on the sofa eating chips wasting the time we have. We must stay hungry and curious about what the possibilities hold for us and manifest our thoughts into reality. This creates new and exciting environments and economies to live in and enjoy.

Question #4: Is it to provide ourselves and the ones we love with the basic necessities?

The Squirrel Method: Not only do they create their own environments, but they also create a surplus. Squirrels always hoard their food in case the winter season is longer than expected. They always make multiple homes in case other intruders scare them off. They always use the resources they have to provide their necessities and more.

Most Americans can barely afford the necessities, let alone create a surplus to save and use to invest in areas to create wealth. Most of the time they are only concerned with their present circumstances instead of planning what they need to do in the present to improve their future.

Either you have to cut down on your spending or you need to earn more income if you're going to create a surplus. That's the only two things to improve. Spend less or earn more. A surplus is always needed in order to navigate around and through obstacles that will inadvertently get in your way. You need a surplus of all your resources including money, time, and energy in order for it to work.

How can you create more money? Do you need to learn more skills that companies are hiring for? Do you need to work more hours? Do you need to utilize the skills you currently possess in a different way? Do you need to be creative and create products or services that the marketplace needs and will pay for? In other words, how can you create value? Value that people will pay for giving you a surplus for you and your family to invest in your future?

What about time? How can you create more time? Can you be more productive? Can you delegate? Can you hire people to free up the busy work that weighs you down? Can you combine activities so that multiple things get accomplished at once? There's always ways to create more time so that you can bring more of your unique talents and abilities to our society.

Finally, energy. How will you create a surplus of energy? Just like time, maybe you can combine different activities so you can get a bunch of things accomplished at once. Maybe you ask for help. Maybe you say no to things that take up time and energy without furthering your cause. You're looking for a surplus here, not the bare necessities. In order to do that, you've got to spend the majority of your energy on things that accomplish your surplus, not take away from it.

How you're going to do these things, we will go into detail later in this book. What I want you to start thinking now is how will you start creating a surplus? The exact steps don't matter right now but the open-mindedness to consider it is what matters. In fact, in order for The Squirrel Method to make a contribution to your life and your future, requires you to open your mind to these new ideas and begin to embrace them into your everyday routines.

Question #5: Is it to love?

The Squirrel Method: Squirrels mate and then the males go their separate way. The young will stay with their mothers until they are big enough to venture out on their own. Squirrels learn how to survive and be independent and self-sufficient creatures from their mothers at an early age and aren't surrounded by a family dynamic.

This gives us all hope that love is not necessarily a main purpose for us either. It's a wonderful thing to be in a loving stable relationship, but the most important thing we can learn from the squirrels is that we must not depend on anyone for anything. We must provide what we need ourselves. If we're happy and make a good living, then we can attract a similar mate and start a relationship. But with divorce rates over 50% in this country, having a stable and loving long-term relationship shouldn't be a purpose of living.

Sorry to all of you romantics out there. Being a woman that's been married twice, I can verify that love needs to be first navigated with your mind and then a little heart can go into it. People can sense desperation from others. Dependence on another person, especially when it's concerning basic necessities and finances is an equation for disaster. When you're independent and going through your own personal growth period, you can always find companionship. Like attracts like and lack attracts lack.

Know what you're looking for in a mate and don't settle for someone who doesn't fit the bill just because you're desperate to find someone. Wait and live your life the way you want and happiness will find you. Love will find you. In other words, get your crap together! Don't worry if you haven't been out in a while. You've got more important things to do. You have time, energy, and money to improve these things you dislike about yourself. Take advantage of this precious time that you have now and make those improvements. Once you do that, you'll find that you'll be okay either way, whether love finds you or not.

Question #6: Is it to connect with God or whatever higher spirit you believe in?

The Squirrel Method: Squirrels don't contemplate the universe and their role in it. At least as far as we know it to be true. Squirrels rely on their instincts and act like squirrels. No more. No less. Are their instincts an act of God or the universe? Are their instincts just habitual behaviors their mom taught them when they were babies? Whatever side of the coin you're on, it comes down to one fact. Squirrels are squirrels and they act like no one but squirrels.

Humans, on the other hand, are a little more complex. Have we established our true purpose here on Earth? Often we think about our roles on Earth and if we are a part of God's creation or actually a part of Him. If you believe that we are God's creation, then you believe that you've got one life and that when your body gives up, you die and that's it. It's over. If you believe that you are actually a part of Him, then you believe you are a spiritual entity that's trapped in a physical body. When you die, your spirit or soul is released back into the universe to enjoy and create something new.

It doesn't really matter what you believe in. The fact of the matter is that we have a limited time in the body we are given at this time. At some point our bodies will cease to exist and our life as we know it will die. The question now becomes, what will you do with your life? What will you create and imagine in the rest of your days? Will you be an extra in your movie or will you be the action star front and center controlling what happens in your life. Will you make things happen or allow them to happen to you?

How human will you be? How much unique talent and ability will you foster and contribute to the world? Will you make a difference? Can you make better circumstances for you and other people? How many people can be affected and changed by you? Only you can answer these questions. Only you can be as human as you want to be. No matter how you put it, you must make the most out of the time you're here!

Question #7: Is it to gain knowledge?

The Squirrel Method: Squirrels learn how to be squirrels and survive their environment at an early age by their mothers. Throughout their life, they can also adapt to change in their environments. They have highly developed memories that help them remember where they've buried nuts and seeds. They also figure out how to get into the bird feeders to help supplement their diets. They learn how to avoid danger by using telephone poles and high wires to cross streets so they don't get squashed. They learn how to get under fences to eat out of the garden. They also can detect defects in the nuts they find so they can determine if the nut should be consumed right now or if it can sustain itself for a later date. Squirrels use their basic knowledge and then learn from their environmental changes and adapt their behavior to survive.

Humans do this too, to a certain extent. We start out using our creativity and imagination and then in school we get away from that and start building our intellect and logic. To be able to adapt to our environment, we need to use both our imagination and our logic. We need to think creatively when obstacles get in our way.

Have you ever felt frustrated or even angry when something wasn't turning out the way you wanted? This frustration and anger happens because logic is trying to control a situation that is out of its control. The only thing that you can control is you. Your thoughts and your actions are the only expectations that can be made. Predictability can be assumed when we mimic someone else's actions towards a goal but sometimes outside circumstances occur.

Once we are set in these predictable habitual behavioral patterns, it's sometimes difficult to find new ways of proceeding. It's our comfort zone. It's our subconscious mind taking over and acting in familiar ways. Once these familiar ways are blocked, then we must dig into our logic and imagination again and figure out another way of proceeding.

All the knowledge in the world doesn't matter if it's not paired with imagination. Knowledge will lead you down the path to success, but imagination will help you get around obstacles that you'll find along that path. How you develop and nurture both knowledge and imagination will ultimately be responsible for the wealth and prosperity you and your family can enjoy.

How will you develop and nurture your logic and imagination?

Assignment #1

A. What contributions do you want to make to your family and community?

My answer:

I want to help 10 million people all around the world live a better life. This includes using *The Habit Formula* methodology to change their bad habits and set their   kids up for success, *The Backward Rule* to help them hit their targets, and *The Squirrel Method* to bring wealth and   abundance in all areas of their lives. Through my books, online products, seminars, speaking engagements, and corporate training, I can do just that.

B. What can you do to become self-sufficient and prosperous?

My answer:

I have employed all of these methodologies in my own life and have created wealth by living, within my means, and investing my surplus. I do this by helping others.

C. How can you create your own environment and economy?

My answer:

The more people I help solve their problems, the higher my compensation becomes. I then invest that surplus in real estate that both pays me monthly and also appreciates, growing my investment. My environment consists of positive people that love me and live by the same means as I do. I believe that I control my life and my environment and economy reflect that belief.

D. What are your basic necessities?

My answer:

Material things: house, car, phone, utilities, clothes, food.   Non-material things: travel, love, fun, family and friends.   I keep my life simple, but rich with experience and experiences.

E. How does love play a part in your life?

My answer:

The love of my family and friends mean the most to me. The love of myself is the most important   of all. If I'm not proud of myself and the contributions I give to my community and others, then I haven't done my part and I'm not living to my potential.

F. What role does a higher power (spirit) play in your life?

My answer:

I'm not a religious person per se. But I believe there's a   higher power that everything is made from. I also believe that this higher power flows through all of us and can help us obtain anything we want in our life if we listen and implement its wisdom. I have learned to listen to my inner voice and act accordingly. When I write, I allow this energy to flow through me.

G. What can you learn to improve your position?

My answer:

Listening to others is always a skill that needs to improve. For me to better serve others, I need to listen   to their needs, problems, and concerns. Then I must tap into my own creativity and imagination and come up with a solution to those needs, problems, and concerns. Communicating with others is also an important skill. Being able to effectively communicate your message with someone else is the basis of any successful person or business.

Chapter 2

Get Those Nuts!

The Squirrel Method: Earn it, save it, and multiply it. The main part of the squirrel's life is to provide security for itself. This includes shelter, food, and health. Squirrels don't accumulate money but they do accumulate basic necessities in surplus and these basic methodologies can be transferred to money.

How do squirrels accumulate a surplus? Squirrels learn how to gather food by watching their mother at a young age but also by watching other squirrels once they are adults. They learn the basic law of supply and demand. In the fall when the trees are providing food for them, they kick their hoarding skills into high gear. They know that winter is coming and that in the fall they must collect and store enough food to get them through the winter. This is a basic skill.

Humans need food too, but we don't gather our own food from our immediate environment. We go to the grocery store and get it there. In order to get the food, we need to buy it with currency. Money. Squirrels know that they need more than enough food because there's a shortage coming when the season changes. For some reason, not all of us have this instinct of abundant accumulation.

According to Dictionary.com, abundance means "A very large quantity of something. Plentifulness of the good things in life; prosperity." In other words, what is enough? In order to have enough of the basic necessities to live, we need to have enough money to purchase that prosperity. The U.S. Census Bureau's data from 2018 stated the median income in America was $63,179. Let's break this number down to see if this amount of money can provide abundance and prosperity to our family.

This example is for a husband, wife, and 2 children.

Income: $63,179

Fed Taxes- 12% Rate: $7,581.48

State Tax- 5% Average Rate: $3,158.95

Local Tax- 2% Average Rate: $1,263.58

Total Tax: $12,004.01

Net income: $63,179 - $12004.01 = $51,174.99

Necessities- Conservative Averages:

House/Apartment: $1500/month x 12 months = $18,000

Utilities/Cable/Phone: $415/month x 12 months = $4980

Car/Home Insurance: $200/month x 12 months = $2400

Property Taxes/HOA Fees: $300/ month x 12 months = $3600

Food: $600/month x 12 = $7200

2 Car Payments: $700/month x 12 months = $8400

Total expenses: $44,580

Net Income: $51,174.99 – Necessities: $44,580 = $6,594.99 leftover divided by 12 months = $549.58/ month

We haven't counted entertainment, clothes, vacations, eating out, maintenance on the house, a college fund, an emergency cash fund. Does $550/month sound like an abundance to you?

Of course not!

A better to question to consider is:

What amount of abundance is right for you and your family? All you have to do is break down any income number as I have done previously to see what amount of income will allow you to not only cover your basic needs, but also provide you with abundance or more than you need. Only *you* can determine what that number is but you have to do the math to figure it out. There's only one way of gaining abundance and prosperity. That one word is *increasing*.

Remember abundance means a very large quantity of something. But the word *large* is very ambiguous and not specific. What does the word *large* mean to you? It's all about your perspective. You might perceive $63,000 as a large amount of money if you live in another country like China where the average yearly salary is 63,000 Yan which equates to $8,820 U.S. dollars. Different parts of the U.S. would also increase or decrease the value of that median salary. In some parts of the U.S. you could comfortably live off the median income, where other parts of the U.S. you wouldn't be able to survive. It's all about perspective and context of the income level.

The question we need to ask is:

How much is enough?

The Squirrel Method: Squirrels have a basic instinct to let them know how much is enough. Not only do they collect food constantly, but they also collect a surplus of food and they store it safely until they need it. They collect so much that they forget where they store it and help contribute to our forest growth from the nuts they leave buried in the ground.

How will you earn enough money that not only can you provide the basics for survival for you and your family, but also have so much abundance that you can help contribute to your community and various charitable organizations? To give back and pay it forward, so to speak, is a very special way to live.

Squirrels don't rely on one source of food. They don't rely on one dwelling. They don't stash their food in one spot. Their mentality is that of getting more and of planning for the unknown future. How can we use *The Squirrel Method* in terms of money? In order to do this, let's break down money into core simple terms.

1. What is it?

2. What is your belief about it?

3. How can you earn it?

4. How do you plan it?

5. How do you multiply it?

6. How do you hide it?

Question #1: What is money?

In simple terms, money represents both value and energy. Money itself is paper and metal. It's our perceived value of it that gives it energy. It's how we use that energy that gives us the belief of lack or of abundance. Everything has energy. This is Quantum Physics 101. How much value you give it will determine how much energy you give towards it. Money helps to put our lives in order by exchanging it for the necessities of survival. Money helps us quantify and qualify the experiences we have. Riches in life can be quantified by using money and what it represents. That can also be called experience.

Do you want to travel? To see parts of the world that are culturally different from that from which you are surrounded? These are experiences of new environments, cultures, ideas, and people that only money can provide. The world we live in is based on economics which is the production, consumption, and transfer of wealth. We need money in order to buy the things we need to survive. But remember that it's not only the basics that we're striving for. It's a surplus and abundance of life and life's experiences that we're after. This calls for an abundance and surplus of money.

Do you want to live in a beautiful environment? Maybe a beach community, a mountain side retreat, or a busy bustling metropolitan city? All of these environments require certain levels of wealth to enjoy. In some areas, higher levels of wealth are needed in exchange for the privilege. Others not as much. Money, therefore, can help surround us with the environment we want to live in. Safety can also be felt in the right environment. A proper shelter from the elements needs a certain amount of money to acquire it.

What about helping your family or community? If you only have enough money to provide the basics to you or your family, you can't provide monetary support to other people that also need it. Yes, you can provide time and energy, but we're talking about money in this chapter, and to have a surplus of it to give to charitable events, we have to start thinking about money in a different way that maybe we're used to.

Money can also bring about the feeling of security. Of knowing that there's enough for you to survive. We can focus on the concept of increasing it, if we know we have enough of it as a baseline. This creates comfort and decreases our stress and anxiety around it.

Question #2: What's your belief about money?

Your perception and belief about money is directly associated with the amount you've acquired. If you believe that it's scarce, then you will never find any for yourself. If you perceive it to be difficult to earn, then you will always find ways to block the opportunities for increasing it as they come your way. If you believe that only the lucky people have it, then luck will never be yours to enjoy.

Your belief and perception about money typically isn't that of your own. It's usually an amalgam or mixture of all of the people in your environment and who raised you. It's your programming or operating system. It's become a habitual thought pattern that's repeated and developed over time.

If you were brought up in a small town where the main factory where your dad word shut down, laying him off, you would probably have a scarcity, negative belief about money. Your dad may have blamed the government, the foreigners for stealing the jobs away from him, or the rich greedy bastards that owned the factory and moved it for chapter labor so they could make more money for themselves. Experiences with money can certainly form opinions and concrete beliefs about money. This holds true for anything in life whether it be money, health, or relationships.

In order to increase the amount of money you have and earn, you must first start changing your beliefs and perceptions about it.

Myth: All rich people are evil. Money is evil.

Remember that money is just value we place on material objects and experiences in order to survive. Money isn't evil. That's like saying that love is evil or health is evil. Money, love, or health are not evil. They are a state of energy that one can feel and use to experience their lives. It's the people that use that energy for evil things, like war, suppression or mental humiliation that is evil. Money itself is not evil and if you believe that, you will always find a way to avoid it because most people want to live a good life. If you're open to money, believe that great things can come from it, and align your actions towards getting it, money will flourish to you. This creates positive vibrations towards it. Think of all the good things you could do with a bunch of money?

Close your eyes and imagine you won the lottery. The cash prize after taxes is $1 Billion. How would your life be different? Would you become evil and use it to hurt people? Of course not. You'd buy some fun stuff that you always wanted. Then what will you do? You'd probably start helping your family and friends. Then you'd branch out and help your local community. When that was done, you'd probably find a way to create something sustainable that could help even more people, wouldn't you? Once you had enough for yourself, then you'd find ways of helping others. That's what money does! It wants to expand and help others be able to survive and live a great life.

Myth: I don't know anything about money. I'm not good at it.

There's not much to know about money. Money is very simple. Money is energy. Energy is all around us. You don't have to be good at it or know much about it. All you have to do is be open to it and its value and align your actions to receive it. Once you receive it, you then must circulate it so it can be used by other people. That's it! It's not difficult and we are all surrounded by it.

Think of money as a tiny tomato seed. How do you take care of it? You give it a home in some soil and fuel the seed with food and water. Then as the plant grows it starts to flower and eventually gives you tomatoes that you can eat. The seed is like money. You nurture and develop your skills in your particular industry. You network and sell your products and services globally. Then the money you earn from that can help feed you, clothe you, and give you many life experiences you want. It's all the same thing. It's just energy. Yes you need to know the steps in order to take care of that energy, and we will teach you those basic steps throughout this book, but for the most part, it's very simple. The energy and knowledge that tine tomato seed has to grow into a flourishing plant is already inside its structure. The same thing is true with money. You and I already have the energy and knowledge inside our minds to align us with money energy. We have to nurture and develop it so it can grow.

Myth: I can't save any money.

There's two possible problems with this belief. Either they have a spending problem or they have a lack of discipline. Let's address one at a time.

"I don't save money because I need more stuff." Obviously they have a spending problem. They have an emotional tie with money. Their emotional tie with money is that they don't want it. They are constantly giving it to other people in exchange for some type of material object or experience. They feel security in the exchange and the material object. Maybe they fear money and that they will somehow lose it if they don't have any of it. If they will learn how to save it and multiply it, then that fear will dissipate. Knowledge can always trump fear when it's gained.

"I don't save money because I lack the discipline to save it." Discipline is the mind giving itself a command and then the body follows that command. Creating discipline is very easy. It takes focus and time to create it. An easy way to create discipline without even knowing it is to use technology in your favor. If you want to pay off a credit card, use your bank's online portal to set up a weekly automatic payment to the credit card company. Once a month you can pay your usual amount, but in order to pay it off early, you'll have to be disciplined. No problem, let the internet build the discipline for you! Set up automatic payments. If your employer can set up automatic payments too, set it up to contribute to your retirement plan, college savings plan for your children, and HSA account. You won't even see this money and it will steadily grow where you won't disturb it.

Myth: All debt is bad debt.

Debt or lack is negative energy. But sometimes debt must be used as a springboard to create prosperity. Consumer items like retail goods should be paid with cash. If you own a small business and must acquire debt to build your business, this can be considered good debt or good energy. That energy will be multiplied over time when your business takes off and floods the marketplace with your products and services. Using money to buy an overload of material objects to fulfill some kind of emotional need is not okay. Learn how interest can halt the growth of your money?

Remember the tomato plant we referenced previously? If you planted the seed in a tiny container, would it grow? Sure it would. What happens when the plant grows so big that there's roots coming out of the bottom and the plastic container is starting to crack? It needs a bigger container. What happens if you don't replant it in a bigger container? It will die. There won't be any room for growth and the roots will become damaged and the life source that drove the growth of the plant will be gone. Myth: All debt is bad debt.

Debt or lack is negative energy. But sometimes debt must be used as a springboard to create prosperity. Consumer items like retail goods should be paid with cash. If you own a small business and must acquire debt to build your business, this can be considered good debt or good energy. That energy will be multiplied over time when your business takes off and floods the marketplace with your products and services. Using money to buy an overload of material objects to fulfill some kind of emotional need is not okay. Learn how interest can halt the growth of your money?

Remember the tomato plant we referenced previously? If you planted the seed in a tiny container, would it grow? Sure it would. What happens when the plant grows so big that there's roots coming out of the bottom and the plastic container is starting to crack? It needs a bigger container. What happens if you don't replant it in a bigger container? It will die. There won't be any room for growth and the roots will become damaged and the life source that drove the growth of the plant will be gone.

Debt does the same thing to your money energy. Interest acts like the container. It won't allow your money to grow if you're in debt because you will always be paying something out instead of allowing it to multiply and flourish. The only time interest can be a good thing is if it's on your side, not the lending side. I'm talking about compound interest. If you are debt-free, you can use interest to invest in companies and real estate that grow. Their growth provides interest in the form of a dividend that will allow your money to grow. Interest is a wonderful thing, but only if it's used for you and not against you. Make sure you align with it and not against it.

Myth: I'm too young or too old to save money.

Time is something we can't control but it's something we can choose to take advantage of. If you're young, obviously you have more opportunities to earn money. If you're wise, you'll use this time to start creating a surplus of money and invest it in businesses and real estate that will grow. Remember compound interest that we mentioned previously? Interest will always work in your favor if you are on the right side of it (surplus not debt) and give it time to do its magic.

Even if you're older, you still can enjoy the fruits of interest. It's never too late to form a good habit! You can help more people. You can travel and enjoy more experiences. You can even leave a legacy for your own family if you can create the saving discipline. Your age doesn't matter. It's the effort and discipline that does. Remember that money is energy and loves to do work. In order to spread the money around, you have to have a surplus. Think abundance at any age!

Myth: Money makes money. I don't have any, so why bother?

Yes, money can multiply and make other money. But how do you make money in the first place? It's aligning your efforts to acquiring it. It's the selfless efforts to help others solve their problems that will ultimately help you solve your own. In order to have it, you must be open to it. In order to be open to it, you must have a positive attitude towards it. If you don't like money, money won't like you. Learn how to make it, then you too will be able to multiply it.

Myth: I deserve this. My family deserves the best.

Of course you want to give you and your family the best things in life. But you need to really think about what that statement means to you and your family. If you want to take them to Disney but you don't have enough money to have an emergency fund, pay off your credit cards, do you think that's giving them the best? Your best? Teaching your family to live within their means, to sacrifice material goods for future abundance, and for living through experience, not material goods are all great habits of passion. It's always better to plan for the future and not use it all for the present!

Myth: I've got to keep up with my neighbors.

Society can definitely put pressure on you and your economy. The question you need to ask yourself is why do you care? Why do you even care if someone else is driving a Mercedes and you've got a Subaru? Why do you care if your house is only 2000 square feet and your friend's house is 5000? The problem that most people have is they have the wrong perception.

They perceive that material objects mean power and importance. What they seem to forget is that most of those material objects come with an attached amount of anxiety and stress. What's the cost difference between a dented bumper on a Mercedes to fix it compared to a Subaru's? A couple of thousand dollars, depending on the extent of the damage. The more expensive an item is, the more expensive the upkeep is. Do you want this responsibility? Do you want anxiety and stress? These expenses will mean that other life experiences won't be achieved. These expenses will mean that you'll have to continue to work hard to keep them going. Is this what you want? So you can fit in with the other people that can't truly afford this stuff either?

Myth: I will always be broke.

One of my favorite quotes came from Henry Ford. "If you think you can or can't, you're right!" It's the way you think about money that will give you your money results. If you believe you will always be broke, you will always find ways to give it to other people. You will never save it and invest it to force interest to be on your side. You will never find the ambition and motivation to find more of it. You will never be open to receiving it and it will oblige this attitude. You will live the way you believe.

Question #3: How do I earn it?

The Squirrel Method: Squirrels obviously don't have jobs and earn money, but they are very active in their communities.

The Law of Compensation states that you will be compensated for your efforts and contribution. If you give something of value (a product or service) to others, they will then give you something that you value (money) in return.

Earning it is one of the simplest concepts to learn but very few people enforce it. Why? Most people only think of themselves. They ask the employer, "How much are you going to pay me for that?" They don't understand the Law of Compensation. In Wallace Wattles' book *The Science of Getting Rich,* he explains this concept in simple terms.

Give every man more in use value than you take from him in cash value; then you are adding to the life of the world by every business transaction.

In other words, give more value to someone than you are charging for it, and they will pay your price for it. Most people make money. They believe that it's owed to them for some type of work that they perform. Mr. Wattles suggests that if you begin to add value to other people, they will gladly pay you what that value is worth. You can do this by solving someone's problems. Most people will pay to avoid pain. They will pay to avoid a problem or solve it. If you have a leaky pipe on a holiday, for example, you will pay the plumber any price they set in order to get the pipe fixed so you can enjoy your holiday. If you learn your loved one has cancer, you will do everything possible to get them the treatment they need in order to survive.

The Law of Compensation is the same as a garden. You sow a little and you reap a lot. Think of how small that tomato seed is. You put it in the ground, cover it up, fertilize and water it a little, and give it time. After three months, what do you find? A huge plant with a bounty of fruit or veggies to harvest. The energy in that tiny seed was nurtured and it exploded and expanded into something hundreds of times its size.

Money is the same energy. If you nurture it and give it some time, it too will explode and expand into hundreds of times its size. The energy and effort you put into solving your customer's problems with new products and services can multiply your wealth vastly. The concept is simple, but the implementation is what stops most people.

Most people want instant gratification and compensation. "I worked my 40 hour week, I want my paycheck." So what do they get? Their 40 hours a week paycheck. Nothing more, and nothing less. How can that employee earn more? It's easy. By finding a need in the company to fulfill. Is the company running short in something? Is there a lack in a department of skill or labor? Can you help your department become more efficient and drive productivity through the roof? You must start thinking of others and their problems before you focus on yourself.

When you do this, you can create a boomerang effect. Energy put out into the Universe always wants to come back to its source. If you're putting forth more effort and are constantly using your creativity to solve your company's problems, you will be rewarded for that effort. Your company will start to depend on you and your creativity to lead others. For this, they will pay you handsomely.

To gain wealth and abundance is to help other people gain their wealth and abundance first. This tells others that you are putting forth effort and compassion to help them. People are drawn to others they like and feel connected to. To help others, you must be unique and creative. You must also stand firm on that uniqueness and creativity and share it with as many people as possible. This expression always causes you to be on offense and control your environment and what you bring to the marketplace. Being on offense also allows you to remain positive and optimistic that you can help other people. You can fuel your ambition and imagination when the compensation for your efforts start to roll in. It's a giant snowball effect. It's like the tiny seed we mentioned prior. It explodes and expands and opens doors to other opportunities for growth. It creates magnetism in you. More people will want to be around you because you can make things happen. This means you can improve everyone's lives. Who doesn't want that?

This attitude towards helping others first is in contrast to the attitude of getting my due diligence, isn't it? "I did what was asked of me and I was compensated for that" Tit for tat. This kind of attitude doesn't foster expansion or improvement for anyone. It won't allow you to provide your best efforts or become great. It won't allow you to stretch and strive for more. It won't allow you to increase your wealth because you're doing just enough to get by. And if you're doing *just enough* at work, I can guarantee you're doing *just enough* in other areas of your life too.

The Squirrel Method encourages you to think abundance. Like the squirrels, they are always striving for more. More food, more activity, and more shelter. They don't necessarily share their ambition of abundance with other squirrels (some species do) but they always strive for more by keeping themselves busy and productive.

Solving other people's problems first is the easiest way to earn money.

The Law of Compensation also states that you are able to earn money by your ability to do your job. In other words, how good are you at what you do? You can earn a ton of money if you're the best in your industry. In order to be the best, you must not only train and practice, but you must also get out in the marketplace and test out your skills.

You'll never get good at your chosen career if you sit at home and don't expand your reach. If you're not constantly practicing and honing your skills, you'll never know when an opportunity for business will come across your path. If you're not out in the community, you'll never be able to expand your network and people won't know who and what you do for a living.

Live *The Squirrel Method*. Squirrels are constantly moving around their environments, testing their abilities to walk across telephone and cable wires and moving into unknown and unfamiliar territories. They are always on the hunt for a nut. Be like a squirrel. If that means you must expand your network and reach globally, do it!

We live in an age where connectivity is so easy and so massive. But only the visionaries take advantage of this opportunity. Think of the big companies of the United States in the 1800's. They had no internet. They had limited transportation. Yet, visionaries like John Pemberton, founder of Coca Cola, William Colgate, founder of Colgate, the Pfaltzgraff family, founders of Pfaltzgraff dinnerware, Rowland Hussey Macy, founder of Macy's, and Aaron Burr, founder of JP Morgan Chase saw endless opportunities for their stores and products to change the landscape both in the United States and abroad.

Maybe you don't want to go global with your products or services. That's okay. The question you need to ask yourself is, "How can I flood my community with my name and my products and services?" When you and your products and services become well-known in your area, then expansion can become a reality. But you must focus on getting out of obscurity and becoming great at what you do which is part of the Law of Compensation.

In order to be great at what you do, you must train and practice every day. Getting out into your community and honing your skills. Passing along value to anyone that wants it will return you and your business with endless opportunities and endless sales. When you solve people's problems, you will be rewarded handsomely.

Question #4: How to plan it?

The Squirrel Method: Squirrels are always busy. You never see a squirrel watching TV or relaxing in the sun. They are always being productive either searching for food, storing it, or creating shelters. Squirrels live between six to eighteen years depending on their species and environments. They don't waste time and they certainly don't waste energy. Their instincts kick in as the weather changes. They know a shortage of food and shelter will occur and they make the most of the time they have to prepare for the shortage.

We must make a plan for our money too as we earn it. Once we figure out how to earn some, then what? That's where strategic planning must be implemented. This planning is called a budget. I know, yuck a budget. The word budget has gotten a bad rap over the years because everyone wants to have the freedom to live their lives the way they want and a budget prevents that from happening. The wealthy and affluent know that intelligent planning as well as discipline can make or break anyone's bank account.

Budget + Discipline + Saving + Investment + Time = Wealth.

It's a simple formula for wealth, but most people never get past the budget part to make any of it work. According to Dictionary.com, budget means "an estimate of income and expenditure for a set period of time." In other words, how much money is coming in and out. After expenses, what's left? Can any of those fixed expenses be eliminated or decreased so there's more discretionary money to save and invest?

If you get a raise or find a different job paying you more money, what's the smart thing to do with that surplus? No, it's not to buy a bigger house or a better car. No, it's not to take a European vacation or buy some new clothes. Your fixed expenses should not change. The excess you make can now be saved and invested. Remember we talked about compound interest? You can use it to build your wealth by giving it time to multiply. Choose investments that are conservative and have a high chance of appreciating so you don't lose all the money you've been diligently saving and investing.

Another way you can make a plan for your money is to minimize the amount of credit cards you have in your wallet. The credit card companies will gladly give you multiple credit cards knowing that there are 189 million cards being used. They also know that there's also over $1 Trillion that are owed to credit card companies so the likelihood that you'll keep spending is rather high.

What these credit card companies don't know is that you're one of the smart people out there and you're learning how to control your debt so you can break free from the masses. That's why you're reading this book, right? An easy way to minimize or even eliminate credit card debt is to only have one card. Choose a card with a rewards or cash-back option. Make sure they have a low interest rate. Only use the card as a last resort.

Pay for all consumer purchases using cash or a debit card. By planning your money this way, you either have enough to make the purchase or you don't. Using credit cards makes purchasing items way too easy. Being cognizant of what you're doing by paying cash or debit is the smart choice to make and can keep you easily on your budget.

The key here is to do everything in your power to stay on your budget. If you can stay out of debt, you can reach your wealth levels easier and quicker. If you're reading this book and you haven't been disciplined enough to stay on your budget, don't worry. I'm here to help. You have to switch your thinking from defensive to offensive. You must get yourself out of debt as soon as possible.

There's only one way to do this, pay more money on the principle than the minimum payments. Paying the minimum payments per month will only keep you indebted to the credit card companies forever!

Here's a few suggestions to help accelerate the process:

1. You must earn more money. Pick up extra hours at work or get a part-time job and designate *all* of that money for debt elimination.

2. Cut out something. Maybe you cut out Starbucks every day. Maybe you pack your lunch instead of eating out. Maybe you put up with your old wardrobe for now and eliminate new purchases.

3. Pay weekly. Instead of waiting for the interest to be calculated on the principle monthly, why not make extra payments weekly? The principle will shrink faster

and the debt can be paid off quicker. You can arrange automatic weekly payments through your bank's online portal.

4. Pay off on credit card or loan one at a time. There's two theories for debt elimination. One is to pay off the smallest debt first. The other one is to pay off the highest rate first. I like the smallest debt method because I can quickly make progress and see results. This creates momentum.

5. Consolidate your debt. Maybe you can take out a HELOC on your home equity and migrate all your debt on one card. Maybe you take out a personal loan to consolidate all of it for one easy payment. Maybe you open a new credit card and transfer all of your debt onto one card. Do your homework and think creatively how you can get your debt in one place for easy pay off.

Remember that money is energy. It's how we control that energy that can create prosperity and wealth for us. If we control money and have a definite plan for it, it can make life easier for us. No one wants to be constantly worrying about money or lack of. Discipline is your mind giving you a command and then your body following that command. Become very disciplined with following your budget and plan for your money.

And because money is energy, it loves to flow. It loves to circulate. But how is it circulating? Are you an endless supply of circulation in and out of your wallet with nothing to show for it? Are you one of those people that get paid on Friday and are broke by Monday with nothing to show for it but a hangover and a risqué video of you and your friends?

Control the flow of money energy or it will control you.

It takes mental strength to say no to friends and opportunities. Fitting in and being trendy are all social pressures that everyone must endure through life. In the end, how do you want to be remembered? As someone who didn't have a clue and with nothing to show for it? Or someone that was prosperous and provided wonderful experiences for their families? Make sure you don't find yourself in the hole and create your money plan today!

Question #5: How to multiply it?

Squirrel Method: Squirrels multiply their stashes by working constantly. They look for a variety of foods like fruits, veggies, nuts, and seeds to help support their longevity. They build multiple shelters in case another squirrel or bird moves in. They have multiple stashes of food. They never rely on one source of anything for their survival.

To save money is one thing. To multiply it is another. In order to multiply money, you must be knowledgeable on how to do it. This is another very simple concept that few people take the time to learn and implement. The only way money can multiply is over time with the creation of more value. Time can make anything more valuable if that value is nurtured.

Investments can make that happen. You can invest in your own business and grow it. You can invest in other businesses and hope that they grow. You can invest in property and raise property values over time to increase appreciation. You can invest in intellectual or artistic products that can create ongoing payments like royalties. There's so many things that can be invested and grown over time. Here's a list of most of them:

Stocks	Bonds
Mutual Funds	ETFs
Retirement Plans	Options
Whole Life Insurance	Forex

Annuities	Land
Private Companies	Songs
Money Markets	CDs
Savings accounts	Art
Precious Metals	Commodities
Jewelry	Rare Coins
Books	Copyrighted Material
Cryptocurrencies	Collectibles
Commercial Real Estate	Tax Liens
Residential Real Estate	Newsletters
Venture Capital	Private Mortgages
Movies	Documentaries
Plays	Amazon Products
Nascar	Sports Teams
Cars	Storage Units
Crowdfunding Projects	Burial Plots

Mineral Rights	HSAs
Oil Wells	Trading Bots

According to Warren Buffett, the two rules of investing are:

1. Never lose money.

2. Refer to Rule #1.

A lot of investment opportunities on the previous list have risk to them. Risk comes down to how much of the risk can you personally control? Can you control a company that you don't own? Can you control your own knowledge on any of these investment opportunities? Can you control how much money you invest and how diversified you are?

The more control you have over your investments will allow you to make strategic moves at various times throughout your life. The key is control. If you've spread out your investments to hundreds of different structures, can you watch it? If you give your investments to someone else, can you control it? Earning it and saving it are one thing while controlling and multiplying it are another.

Keep your money close to you and make sure you understand how it's being used and multiplied. Only then can true wealth be obtained.

You don't have to do it alone. There's a whole industry out there called financial services. Use them. Find someone that has a proven track record as a Certified Financial Planner. These professionals earn their commission on the upswing of your account and nothing more. If you don't make money, they don't either. Do you think these people are interested in your success? Of course. They want to see you do better so that they do better. It's a win-win situation for everyone. These people work independently of the big fund companies like Edward Jones or MetLife. They don't have to "sell" you certain products because they work for that certain company. They can invest you in any or all areas of the market and have the knowledge to help you succeed in your wealth journey.

Do your due diligence before you hand over your hard-earned money to someone else. Make sure this person has your best interest in mind first and then themselves second. Look for opportunities with limited downside exposure and unlimited upside exposure. Yes, those opportunities do exist and the wealthy people have known about them for centuries. Tap into the opportunities that the wealthy tap into and you're sure to find the same future success!

Question #6: How to hide it?

The Squirrel Method: Squirrels are notorious for scattering their stashes in hundreds of places. So much so, that they often forget where all of their stashed goods are and single-handedly help to replant our forests. Mikel Delgado, a grad student at UC Berkeley studied the daily habits of squirrels and noticed that not all food got stashed for the winter. Squirrels had the innate ability to question their food's perishability and nutritional value and would decipher what to hide based on these observations. They often would "pretend" to buy nuts in one spot, only to bury them in another in fear that they were being watched.

The financial advisors in the modern age tell us to do the same thing with our investments and retirement plans. They tell us to buy investment vehicles that average out the market over entire sectors or indexes. Don't put all of your eggs in one basket, right? We've all heard that quote. The problem with this theory is that it's very difficult to watch your "stash of nuts" when it's spread out too thin. Being *too* diverse can lead you to forget or neglect an investment that could cause it to be depleted. Some different advice I've heard came from Andrew Carnegie who said that you should put as much as you can in one basket and then watch that basket like a hawk!

Of course, that was during the Industrial Revolution when huge industrial corporations were being grown. I'm not sure that advice holds 100% true today. If you own a business, then it will be necessary for you to put a lot of your own capital into your own business to help it grow.

The question is, "What do you do when you're starting to make more money than you need?" This is when knowledge of how to multiply your money comes back into play. Everyone's biggest expense is taxes. Not only do you have to multiply your money, but you also have to know what tax implications go with that multiplication. There are numerous vehicles in the market that grow after-tax dollars and can help you grow your nest egg without the fear of paying future higher taxes when it's time to start using that money. Most vehicles that pay dividends are taxed at lower rates than earned income.

Another concern you need to think about are the fees and rules that go along with those investment vehicles.

Are there penalties involved for early withdrawal? What are the management fees? Are there required distributions? At what age? Are there limitations in the amount you can invest depending on your health or income? Are you guaranteed a dividend? How often are you paid those dividends? Can you automatically reinvest those dividends? Can the vehicle lose its value?

What are the risks of this investment? I still don't understand the popular concept of taking more risk when you're young to take advantage of the time and compound interest factor. You should be just as conservative when you're young. Remember Warren Buffett's saying of not losing money? If you risk your money when you're young and lose it, you can't take advantage of time and compound interest when you don't have any money to grow. It's gone. You should always be conservative with your money and not risk it on *maybe's* and *could-be's*.

The question in this section is twofold. How do you hide your money so others (like the IRS) can't get to it and how do you hide your money so *you* don't squander it? These are two very good subjects that we must cover in order for you to have financial freedom. Let's tackle the second one first.

How do you hide your money so *you* don't squander it?

Saving money is a disciplined action. Most people buy things based on emotions. "Ooo, I want that." "Wow! That would look great on me." "I wish I had that, you know what? I deserve it, I'll take it." The discipline of saving money requires you to shut out the emotional wants and commands you to think rationally about the purchase in front of you. You must have a rational mindset of what's most important to you. Will buying those boots get you closer to financial freedom? Of course everyone needs a pair of boots, that's not what this is about.

What it's about is having multiple pairs of boots. When you're trying to save money, build wealth, and get rid of debt, multiplying the way you spend your money is *not* the objective. The objective is to live life frugally and sacrifice your wants in the present for the celebration of your wants in the future.

I know, *frugal* and *sacrifice* are two very ugly words. According to Dictionary.com, frugal is, "Sparing or economical with regard to money or food. Simple and plain and costing little." Think of living frugally by simplifying your life. This can mean minimizing material objects that can only clutter your life and strap you down in debt. If simplicity is established, the conscious rational mind can focus its attention on one simple idea, build wealth. If your conscious mind is constantly battling with the emotional subconscious mind on every little thing, it can't help you think clearly on your main objective of building financial freedom.

The same can be true for the word sacrifice. According to Dictionary.com, sacrifice means, "An act of giving up something valued for the sake of something else regarded as more important or worthy." Isn't financial freedom and an unlimited possibility of wealth worth a little sacrifice today? I know it's difficult to not fit in because your wardrobe needs a little upgrading or your couch is falling apart. But if you first discipline yourself and live debt-free and *then* you save your money to invest, you will look back on those frugal sacrificing years and say that those few years were the turning point of your success.

The second part of the question is:

How do you hide your money so others (like the IRS) can't get ahold of it?

All of the concepts we're going to mention next are all legal loopholes and strategies the wealthy people use to keep and multiply their wealth. This also includes paying little to no tax on any of it. How is that possible?

Remember who runs this country. Most Congressmen and politicians who make the laws are also ones that directly benefit from those same laws. How can you use these strategies too?

It's quite simple. You have to know about them first and then you must be disciplined enough to save your money so you can invest in them too and use the *Laws of the Land* in your favor. Here's some examples. Make sure to check with your accountant and financial advisor for more creative loopholes that you can legally fall through to save on your tax bill.

Method #1: Own a Business

Even if it's a simple LLC, owning your own business has significant tax savings. For instance, there are numerous deductions for things like vehicles, office supplies, materials and goods, personal development, travel, and insurance. There's FICA deductions which are taken out up to a certain amount and then they are phased out giving you more take-home pay. If you own your business 100%, you can pay yourself dividends that aren't subject to normal income tax or FICA. You can purchase equipment for the business and depreciate the cost of the equipment either all in one year or spaced out over consecutive years. If you have a decent accountant, they can help you deduct all the costs that small business owners are privileged.

Method #2: Dividends

Any investment that is made will then hopefully appreciate and grow in value. The growth is that value of the business or real estate and can be paid not only in value but also as a dividend. Dividends are taxed by the IRS in the lowest tax bracket making them cheaper income than any earned income on the planet. This is what makes real estate and private companies so appealing. The investments are used with post-tax dollars in the earned bracket amount and then the dividends are taxed on the lower tax bracket. It's a great concept to employ! Nothing else can grow your nest egg faster than through the dividend method.

Method #3: Real Estate

This method can supercharge your wealth and use the IRS rules to its fullest. Investment real estate, whether it's single family homes, land, commercial, or residential multi-family properties can be purchased or invested with post-tax dollars. Any repairs or upgrades to the properties can be deducted. Any interest from the purchase loans can be deducted. As the rents go up, the appreciation of the property also goes up because it has an inflow of income that's increasing while the debt is coincidently being paid from those same rents.

Once the down payment is returned through the property appreciation, the property can either be sold or refinanced returning the original down payment to the owner plus any money that's been paid on the original debt. The proceeds from the sale or refinance *cannot* be taxed in most cases. Some investments need to be reinvested in more property to follow the tax rules, but some do not. These are the ways the wealthy increase their net worth significantly. This is also the way that beginners use the IRS rules to break into the wealth ranks. If you know the rules, you can always take advantage of them. If you don't, you won't. It's as simple as that!

Method #4: Whole Life Insurance Policy

This method utilizes post-tax dollars to provide a vehicle not only for growth over time, but also an insurance death benefit that can provide for your family if you're not around. A whole life policy guarantees you a certain percentage of growth in any market plus a percentage of growth on the upside of the market. The insurance premiums can be set to automatically use the dividends to pay for themselves at a certain point in time. The owner of the policy can then use the cash value of the policy as it grows and loan themselves money. This money can be used to buy a car or as their retirement stipend. No dividends or capital gains can be taxed as these investments are considered loans between you and the insurance company and don't even need to show up on your tax forms as income. They're taxed once in the beginning before investing and grow tax free from there. Many upper middle class and wealthy individuals set these plans up and use them as retirement options because you're guaranteed growth, even in a down market. You also get a death benefit and there's no tax on capital gains.

Method #5: Fixed Index Annuities

Fixed index annuities give you the opportunity to earn returns based on the performance of a stock index, like the S&P 500 without the risk of ever losing money in a year when the stock market declines. They have guaranteed minimum earnings and a share of the upside.

Some people think of these plans as personal pensions. They can also be called equity annuities. These plans are usually offered through insurance plans. They are investments that are insured, and they are linked to the interest rate. This means that the interest paid on these annuities will be affected by the stock market index. As long as the stock market index rises, your account will be credited by the insurance company, with their cut coming out of the credit. If the index falls, however, your insurer will protect your investment against any possible loss through a positive rate of interest. If the market has a negative year, you will not lose any money from your principal, and you will not earn any interest payments.

These have been popular investment tools over the past decade because you have a share of the upside and no penalties on the downside. You simply don't lose money as the markets fall. However, make sure that you know what the management fees are because they can drastically differ and can hinder the growth of your investments.

Method #6: Health Savings Account

Health Savings Accounts (HSA) have become popular over the last few years as the premiums for ObamaCare health insurance plans skyrocketed. For self-employed people, staying on ObamaCare plans became difficult because of high premiums and even higher deductibles. This forced most small business owners to look for other ways to pay for their health care needs.

HSA's do just that. They provide not only a way to save yearly for unexpected health care costs that the insurance policies wouldn't cover, but they also provide a way to use the money that wasn't utilized for healthcare costs and invest it into products that could grow that money over time. Unlike a flexible savings account which has funds that need to be used before a certain date or they go away, the health savings account funds can accumulate tax-free year after year.

Funds can grow tax free and can be withdrawn tax free as long as they are spent on qualified medical expenses including deductibles and copayments. Like other investment products, when you die, you can transfer the funds left in the HSA to a listed beneficiary. If you want to use the funds in other ways during retirement, they would be subject to your income tax rate.

Summary

Most wealthy people use any or all of these methods to use the rules of the IRS in their favor. Why don't you think Mitt Romney or President Donald Trump wanted to release their financial statements to the public? Probably because it would turn off voter support when they found out these guys paid less tax than you and I did! It's not that they did anything illegal, either. They were smart enough to use the rules of the IRS to benefit them and their families.

They owned their own businesses with massive deductions. They owned countless amounts of real estate properties that enjoyed appreciation and deductions. And I'm sure they used whole life policies to stash and grow cash that the IRS couldn't get ahold of.

To become wealthy, you must use every resource at your disposal. This includes investment vehicles that can be taxed too and grow in value. Knowledge in tax law is by far the most superior way to grow multi-generational wealth. You don't have to know the entire tax code, just the sections that pertain to growing wealth with few conditions. Hiding your money doesn't mean doing anything illegal. Hiding it means to invest it in vehicles that have special IRS rules that benefit the investor not the IRS. Use these vehicles and watch your wealth grow.

Make sure you talk with a qualified investment and tax specialist before investing in any of these vehicles and do your due diligence. No one will ever care about your money more than you do! Make sure you know how you're going to multiply your money and what tax advantages are out there before you invest in any strategy.

Assignment #2

This exercise is meant to challenge your beliefs in money so you can get past the lies you're telling yourself and your family about money. If you can get past these lies, you can start working on your future wealth and prosperity that could change the tides of your family history for generations to come.

Answer the following questions truthfully. Once you've answered them, challenge yourself on how you can change these beliefs. Will your beliefs create wealth for you? Are your beliefs holding you back? How will you change them and create a different path to follow?

Questions

1. How much money do you earn per year?

2. How much money do you save per year?

3. What investments do you have?

4. How much money is "enough" for you to live comfortably? (This number is probably too low.)

5. How much money is "enough" for you to feel like you're rich?

6. Do you believe you deserve to be wealthy and prosperous?

7. Do you believe all rich people are evil?

8. Do you believe all money is evil?

9. Do you believe you're no good at the money thing?

10. Do you believe you can't save money?

11. Do you believe that all debt is bad?

12. Do you believe you're too young or too old to save money?

13. Do you believe that money makes money so why bother?

14. Do you believe I deserve to buy anything I want?

15. Do you believe you must keep up with the neighbors?

16. Do you believe you will always be broke?

To flip your beliefs around and allow your subconscious mind to start moving you into a new world, answer the following:

17. How can I earn more?

18. What's my plan for my money in the future?

19. How can I multiply my money?

20. What vehicles can I use to legally hide my money from the taxman?

Chapter 3

The Car's Coming- Move It!

The Squirrel Method: Squirrels can live up to 18 years depending on the species and their environment. Their entire lives are spent working on food storage and building shelters. They are always planning their futures by being fully present in the moment and doing as much as they can in their present time. You never see a squirrel sunning themselves or taking a nap in a tree. They are always working towards their survival.

This chapter is fully dedicated to building your awareness of your present condition. You're never going to find your nuts and get rich if you don't know where your starting point is. Where are you right now? What actions are you taking? What thoughts do you have? Do you have a plan for the day? Are you executing that plan? Are you busy or are you productive? Are you being efficient with your time or are you wasting it? Do you finish your projects today or are you procrastinating or waiting for the right time or situation to occur?

In order to answer these questions, let's back up a moment and define what the word awareness is. According to Dictionary.com, awareness is, "The state of being aware, having knowledge, or consciousness." The only moment in time that awareness plays a role is in the present moment. Now. It's the moment in time when all your thoughts and actions come together. When you make a decision to carry out a movement or action.

Now is the most powerful time in history. The present time can completely form what the results will be in the future. If you don't control the present time, you can never be in control of the future and its results. If you don't commit your resources into making this time, now, as productive as possible, the future results can be harmed.

How do you control the present? According to Dictionary.com, control means, "To exercise restraint or direction over; dominate; command." In other words, you've got to be in charge of everything in your life in order for you to be in control.

This means your thoughts. This means your actions. This means your resources of time, energy, and money. This means your environment. This means the people in your environment. If you don't control these things now, will you ever be able to control them in the future?

Most of us waste our present time doing mundane busy work that has nothing to do with creating wealth, health, or purpose. We think that we must do certain things to create a certain image of ourselves or to impress our peers. These thoughts couldn't be further from the truth. The problem that most of us have is that we lack a purpose. Without a purpose, we aimlessly move about our day and have no idea where the time goes or how it's spent.

Let's take a look at the word purpose. A purpose is a reason for living. Why are you here? Why are you reading this book? What do you intend to get out of this? Most people read books or take classes because they want to learn some snippets of wisdom that they can then use in their own life to change something or get a different result.

Most of the time, we learn something and then the next day, we forget it and all of the wisdom and experience of that guru is lost forever. Why? One of the main reasons is there's no *implementation* of the information. It's one thing to learn something, it's another thing to start using it and enforcing it in our own lives. But without implementation of this information, our lives are taken over again by the busy mundane work that surrounds us and nothing new ever gets done.

Have you ever bought an online training course or ebook and didn't finish it? Maybe you started it and then something in life pulled you away from your studies and you never returned to it. Why did you buy it in the first place? To learn something that could further your potential? To learn something that would give you a leg up in your market? To learn a new way of doing something that's not available in your market right now?

It's probably all of these things or you wouldn't have purchased the course. But just like anything, if you don't return to your training course, that information is out of sight, out of mind. You forgot about it. You forgot about its importance to you and your future. It's out of your awareness and is sitting in your inbox waiting to be consumed.

I've done this. I've bought numerous training courses over the years to start them and never finish them, let alone, never actually implement them into my daily routines, which is why I bought them in the first place. I allow them to fester and take up room on my computer instead of taking up room in my life and how I run my businesses.

That's why the present time, the now, is so very important to be aware of and to start taking action on. It's the present time that will ultimately create the future. If that new knowledge would be implemented, step by step, into our present time immediately, we can see a change for the better.

When you can control your present time and implement as much activity in the direction of your goals, you'll find that you can obtain your results easier. You then will have experience and the knowledge that you can get around obstacles which will snowball your career and ultimately your life!

The present time is the most important thing we can become aware of. The way we will become aware of what's going on in our present time and how we can control it will be discussed thusly. Let's start answering the earlier statements on building your awareness of your present condition.

Question #1: Where are you right now?

Your awareness uses your five senses to help it orient its presence in its environment. What are your senses telling you about your present condition? Are you cold? Where are you right now? What are you seeing, feeling, smelling, hearing, or tasting? Is your environment pleasant? Is this a place where you spend a lot of time? Can the things and people in this environment help you achieve your goals?

Being aware of how you spend your time, will help you plan on being in an environment that will perpetuate progress and success. If you're spending hours in front of the TV eating chips, that won't help you lose weight and become healthy. If you are spending time at a job that pays very little and takes up a lot of your resources, that won't help you further your family's wealth and prosperity.

Time is one of those things that people tend to take for granted until it's taken away from them. They have a health concern that can dramatically shorten their lifespan. Someone that they love dies suddenly and they realize they wasted a lot of time not reinforcing their purpose with that deceased person. The resource of time is a luxury until it's taken away.

Let's take a look at another resource; money. If you're spending your money on things that aren't important, you like them, but they won't further your life, then why are you wasting your money on those things? Are you even aware that you spent this money today? We talked about this earlier, most people get paid on Friday and wonder where all their money went by Monday. Too many people think that *Payday* Friday means that it's party time and shopping time. There's no fiscal responsibility. There's no awareness of a budget. There's no purpose to their money other than giving it to other people.

"Pay yourself first," is a saying that middle class people ignore and wealthy people live by. "Paying yourself first," means that you have a commitment to not only setting aside a certain amount or percentage of your paycheck every week but that you're going to invest it so that it can multiply over time. Remember what I said before, "Time is a luxury until it's taken away." People that can retire without worry and leave money for their children and grandchildren are people that don't waste time nor money.

These people spend their time on ways to earn, save, and invest more so that they can help their churches and communities when they slow down in their later years. They are fully aware that the present time is such a precious time that they can make wise decisions about their finances so that they can enjoy them later.

Let's talk about goals for a moment. Effort must be placed on slowing down your thoughts and actions and concentrating them on important tasks that need to be done to further your goal achievements. If you can't control your present, you certainly won't be able to control anything else. Control is the most important thing you can do to grow and improve your life.

In order to have control of your life, you must be aware of what you're doing with it. That begins with the present time. If you can control what you're doing right now, you can take whatever actions are needed to improve your life. If you can control how you spend your time, you can concentrate as much activity into as little of time as you can and achieve big things.

What about the people in your life? Are they contributing to your success or not? Sometimes you must control the people that you surround yourself with. Have you heard the saying, "You are the sum of the five people you hang out with?" This is a true statement. If the people in your environment don't care about earning more money, about saving and investing in their future, or improving their skills so they can dominate their markets, do you think you will? Do you think these people will be hanging out, drinking beer, and discussing their investment portfolios? Or role-playing on how to handle their common objections? Of course not! They'll be talking about who has what car or who is dating who or what they're going to eat that night. They're not discussing deep issues or helping one another succeed. They keep things very shallow and never contribute anything to the group that's worthwhile.

Obviously, these people can be your friends, but do you really want to spend a lot of time with them? What exactly are you getting out of these friendships? Fun? A hangover? Memories? Maybe. Or maybe you're afraid to meet new people because the old ones are familiar? Sometimes old friends need to stay in the past if they prevent you from growing into the future. I've had to learn this lesson myself over the years and now spend my time with people that have the same mission as I do and can help me grow as a person and as a business owner.

At some point, you'll have to ask yourself if your environment and the people in it are contributing to your success or hindering it? Once you've answered that question, then you'll have to make up your mind what you're going to do about it. More than likely you'll make the decision to break free from those people and find a new crowd that can improve your life rather than waste it.

Question #2: What actions are you taking?

I'm not asking what actions you *want* to take. I'm not asking you what actions you took yesterday. I'm asking you what you are doing *today*, right now as you're reading this page? Are you working on any of your goals right now? Are you slacking off? Are you doing busy work that doesn't matter? Are you doing things for other people and forgetting your own goals and desires?

When you're aware of what you're actually doing right now in the present time, you can concentrate your efforts on taking actions that matter. If these actions are working towards your goals, awesome! If they aren't, you've got to ask yourself if they are actions worth taking. Why would you waste your resources on actions that don't matter? Ones that won't improve your life, right? Ones that won't put more money in your pocket.

Pay attention to how you're spending your resources. You only have so much energy to exert each day. Make that energy count with the actions you're taking.

Focus your attention on what activities improve your health, your wealth, and your environment. Again it's your focus, your attention, and your plan of attack that determines what you get accomplished today.

You only have so much money to spend on things. Take care of the fixed costs first: food, shelter, clothing, health, and savings. The rest needs to be budgeted carefully so that there's enough to go around when something bad happens. And there will always be something bad that happens. I know, I said the word *budget*. Yuck, right? Most people hate to budget anything, but if you want your money to be spent on things that will help you accomplish your goals, you need to put yourself and your household on a budget.

Ask yourself if the boots that you're going to spend your hard-earned money on is worth the price you're paying. What value are you getting from that purchase? Is it a weekend gratification only? Is it because your other boots have a hole in them and aren't useful? What's the main motive for this purchase? Will these boots make you more money so you can invest more and have a better future? The answer is, probably not.

Anytime you decide to spend money, ask yourself those questions. Really be aware of how you're spending your money and if that purchase is worth all the time, energy, and crap you had to go through. If it is, then go for it. But most of the time you'll decide that it's really all about peer pressure and trying to fit in and it has nothing to do with creating the future that you want.

The younger you start asking yourself these questions and becoming smart and frugal with your money, the easier and sooner your wealthy future will appear. Remember the compounding effect? If you can watch what you spend and invest as much as you can to multiply your money, you can take advantage of the time factor. If you're stupid and frivolous with your money when you're young, you will not be able to take advantage of time.

Speaking of time. What about your time? We are all blessed with the same 24 hours a day. After sleeping eight hours and working eight hours, that leaves another eight hours to spend with the family and take care of the house. But that doesn't necessarily take eight hours to accomplish. There's at least one to two hours (or more) in that eight-hour span that can be used to work on your goals, both personal and professional.

When you use your resources wisely, you can accomplish a lot more than you realize. But you must control how you use them and control who you give them to. Once control is accomplished, a new reality will be felt.

We talked earlier about being aware of how you're spending your money. If you can prioritize your money, you can spend it wisely and know *exactly* how it's being spent. One simple question you can ask yourself is, "Does this person or thing deserve my hard-earned money?" Face it, you've worked hard and long to earn the money that's cashed every week. How do you want to spend that money? Would you rather spend it on another pair of boots when you already have 20 other pairs you can select from? Or would you rather invest that money and multiply it for your future and then buy a new pair of boots? Are the present-time boots more important than your future-time boots? Only you can answer that question. But I dare you to make the right choice. I dare you to choose and act in a way that will allow you to have affluence and integrity that you can share with your community and future generations of your family.

What other goals do you have? To take a vacation? To get in shape? To have a loving relationship? There's more to life than money and material wealth. But they all live harmoniously with each other. If you don't prioritize your time and waste your money on frivolous things, do you think you'll prioritize your energy to being creative or getting in shape? Do you think you'll steer your ambition on learning a new skill set that could land you a new job with a raise and more responsibility? Do you think anyone will be attracted to you when you don't have other areas of your life in order? Probably not.

Make sure you take time every day to focus your resources on you. Your present and your future. Being fully aware of how you spend your resources is both exciting and comforting. Controlling the influences in your life is one of the most powerful skills you can ever learn. Make sure you learn that skill as soon as possible as your future security depends on it.

Question #3: What thoughts do you have?

Every success or failure we have starts with thoughts. We think in images. If we can imagine something happening, then we can take the actions necessary to create the reality. If you don't think something is going to happen, it won't. You won't behave in a way to get things moving towards your goals.

Our thoughts are very powerful motivators. If you want something bad enough, you won't allow any obstacles to hinder your progress. But if you're weak-minded, or easily frustrated, you won't believe that success can happen for you.

Squirrels don't think about these things, at least what I am aware of. They are squirrels. They act like squirrels. If there's some food available, they find it, evaluate it, and store it for the future. They don't worry whether there's enough food out there or not. They act in a way to guarantee that they have enough food when it's winter and the rations are scarce.

Doubt and anxiety are killers of success in people. When we doubt that things will happen, we close down our confidence and act conservatively and anxiously. No one improves or grows when in doubt. Don't worry if your action isn't successful today. If you don't quit, you will succeed. You will work and find a way to succeed in your goal achievement.

Keep throwing ideas into the marketplace. You never know when today's ideas are tomorrow's realities! Think about the possibilities that you can create. Think in positive manners. You are important to our society. You can change anything you want if you concentrate on that thought.

Question #4: Do you have a plan for the day?

Everyone should have a 'To Do List.' In *The Habit Formula: Life's Success Equation*, Chapter 5 is all about focusing your attention and energy on the activities that will get you closer to your goal. Whether it's personal or professional (I recommend working on both) the only way you will improve is to focus on the activities you're doing today and make sure they count. If you want to learn how to create good habits to lead a successful life, grab a copy of *The Habit Formula: Life's Success Equation* right now! It will help you learn the *exact* method of creating any good habit.

If you can put a little time into creating a map of where you are and where you want to go, you can then take the steps necessary to get you to your end point. It sounds simple and it really is. Focused attention is all that's needed to put your plan into action. Rome wasn't built in a day, and neither will your goals. It takes time, but time can make you lose your focus on what it is that you truly want. Time can be wasted so easily because we think we have an abundance of it. In actuality, we don't have a lot of time.

No one knows how long it will take them to reach their goals. No one knows how much effort it will take.

But one thing is certain: if you don't have a plan to get there, you'll never get there. It's like driving in your car and not knowing where you're going. After a while, you become frustrated because you've wasted a lot of time and gas going down the wrong roads and you're still not where you want to go. Create your plan by writing a daily action plan.

Question #5: Are you executing that plan?

After creating your daily action plan, then you have to *actually* take the actions. Thoughts are just thoughts. They have to have the energy of action to help them create a new reality. In other words, do something! If you want to eliminate your debt, stop spending your money on junk and use that extra money to pay down your debt! That's a smart action. Maybe one action you take today to eliminate your debt is to pack your lunch and use the money you'd spend on lunch at a restaurant to decrease your debt.

If you find that you're not doing the tasks that you've written on your plan or you've failed to continue to write up a plan, you've got to ask yourself why you're not working on your plan. Why are you allowing distractions or other people to hinder your progress towards your goals? Is it them or is it you? Are you disciplined and committed to making this change? Is your motivation important enough to you that you will continue to push yourself and your limitations so that you can see improvements in your life?

I know it's hard. I know it takes time and energy to continue on your path to success. But aren't you worth all of the sacrifice? Isn't your family worthy of a better life that you can help provide them? Aren't you sick and tired of being sick and tired? If so, then you've got to pull up your big pants and get to work.

Not every day is going to be successful. Sometimes you're sick. Sometimes obstacles will get in your way. That's okay. That's life. But if you keep pushing and keep focusing your attention and your effort on your goals and on your dreams, it will happen to you. Your life will start to improve. You'll start getting some wins. And then the wins will get closer and closer together to the point that all you're doing is winning and making money and living the life you've always wanted.

But in order to have what you want, you must have a plan to get there and try your damndest to stay on that plan no matter what or who gets in your way! You've got to get back on track when you fall off. You must figure out how to get around that obstacle when it's blocking your progress. Keep pushing through all of the gates and you will find the results that you're looking for. Stay on track. Stay on your plan and complete your daily tasks.

Question #6: Are you busy or are you productive?

Being busy and being productive are two different things. Everyone can fill their day with mundane activities that don't amount to anything useful. Have you ever looked at the clock and wondered where the day went? Most of us have had that experience. The question is:

What did you do during that particular day?

Did you work on activities that got you closer to your goal or did you use your time and energy on distractions? Distractions are a goal killer in everyone's lives. They can rob you of your resources. They can rob you of your time. They can hinder your progress towards living a life of abundance.

If you can work on your daily action plan, you can use your resources wisely and move your life circumstances towards security. Security makes you feel safe. Security can release your restrictions and unleash your creativity.

If you feel like you're not getting anywhere significant in your life, it's probably because you're not doing anything to move it towards the goals you've set. You've got to accomplish something important. You've got to make a difference in your life. You've got to take control of your resources and use them to your benefit and not squander them or give them to other people to use.

If you can accomplish the tasks on your daily action plan, then you are being productive. If you're working your plan and you notice that the day is already gone, then you're moving in the right direction towards security. This doesn't mean that you can't have fun. This doesn't mean that you shouldn't work on house projects, or enjoy your kid's soccer game. What this does mean is that you need to make a daily action plan and then act on that plan.

Without action, nothing will get done. However, most people have limited resources of time, energy, and money. Most people have to work on their action plans little by little and not all at once. This is fine. What keeps most people from wealth and living a healthy, abundant life are the distractions that come into it.

Saying "no" is one of the most powerful and self-liberating things you could say. When you say "no," you are freeing the hold that the distractions around you have on you. You are focusing your attention on the life you want and not on other people and things that could rob you of it. Saying "no" provides the strength you need to accomplish your goals. If you say "no" to something, it will free up your resources in order to say "yes" to something else. It's called priorities.

Prioritize how you spend your resources. Yes, you can give them to other people and activities as long as the majority of them go towards you and your future. If you accomplish your daily action plan first, you can then enjoy what's left of your resources free and clear. Without the guilt that you will feel if you squandered them and accomplished nothing.

Question #7: Are you being efficient with your time or are you wasting it?

Productivity and efficiency go hand in hand. You can become more productive and hit your goals faster if you're more efficient. According to Dictionary.com, efficiency means, "To be able to accomplish something with the least waste of time and effort; competency in performance. The accomplishment of or ability to accomplish a job with a minimum expenditure of time and effort.

In other words, to maximize efficiency is to maximize resources. The question is: how?

Can you do more in a shorter amount of time? You can create more time if you eliminate distractions. You can use all of your energy for the day on accomplishing one activity. This creates a concentrated amount of effort and focus on that one activity. It's like a laser. A laser is powerful because its energy is concentrated in a very small amount of space. There's no wasted space for its potential energy to go. The energy follows the beam and that's where all of it goes. How can you concentrate your energy in one specific area today?

Can you get help doing your project? Maybe you need to hire another person to help you. Maybe your hubby can take some of the burden from you. When there's more energy being put into the task at hand, then you can get more done in a shorter amount of time.

You can also use money to create more time and energy. Can you pay for a babysitter for the day? If so, that time and energy can be placed on accomplishing an activity that can move you towards your goal. Can you pay someone to clean your house? This can free up some time and energy so you can concentrate on making money, working on a project, or working on your health.

You can also be more efficient by delegating. You don't have to do everything. Even if you're not the boss at work, you can still delegate activities that don't move you towards your goals to someone else. Your kids can help you with the chores. Your spouse can take the kids to their practice so you can finish a project. Your coworker can help you find data points so you can keep the project on track. Delegation is a powerful tool that everyone has in their toolbox to help them become more efficient and productive.

Setting deadlines is another way to be more efficient. If you give yourself a deadline to hit your goal or to complete a task or project, you're helping to focus your attention and your energy on accomplishing that task. When you know there's a definite endpoint to something, you can use your resources wisely to move you towards the end point. Motivation occurs when an endpoint is drawing near. It creates urgency. It creates a definite plan. It draws your attention and concentration on accomplishing the deadline. Deadlines work. If they didn't, they wouldn't be used by all the successful companies. Use them in your personal life too and see how efficient you become at hitting your targets.

Organization can also play a role in efficiency. If you're constantly looking for lost items, then you're wasting resources. If things are organized, you can easily find them when they are needed. Being organized is definitely a skill. It takes discipline and persistence to put the files back in the same place every time. It takes discipline and persistence to put the tools back in the garage in their cases. It takes discipline and persistence to put your keys and wallet in the same place every time you come back home. Without organization skills, efficiency can't be found.

Question #8: Do you finish your projects today or are you procrastinating or waiting for the right time or situation to occur?

Procrastination is a killer of productivity and efficiency. Most people are lazy. They don't want to accomplish the things that they need to accomplish in order to become prosperous. That's why the rich get richer and the poor get poorer.

Being wealthy doesn't have anything to do with being intelligent or being popular. Being wealthy and living an abundant life has to do with productivity and efficiency. Where's your motivation? Where's your action plan? Why are you putting off any activity for another time?

This entire chapter has been about the power of now. The present. Nothing is in your direct control but the present. You can control your future and what it looks like if you can control your present. The present is what feeds the future. It's like a fork in the road. You choose your side to travel. You take a step and then another and then another. At first, no matter which direction you take, you are close to the other side of the road. But with time, you will find that the other side has gotten further and further away from your present spot. That's your future. One decision can have massive results in the future.

Time is the leveling factor. Everyone has the same amount of time per day, per week, per month. How are you spending that time? Are you being productive and efficient in it? Or are you wasting it doing mundane activities that will never get you and your family ahead.

Being in control of the present and the thoughts and activities that you are having right now go hand in hand with the awareness of the situation. If you're aware that you have limited time or there's a deadline to accomplish that activity or project, then you will move into action. Without the motivation and the awareness of the need for action, nothing will be accomplished.

People plateau in life because they lose their urgency. Young people especially lose focus easily because they know that they have their whole life ahead of them. So they slack. They are lazy. They feel no motivation to accomplish anything. What they don't realize is that they are in direct control of their future. It's like the fork in the road. Through time, the difference in the path taken can be experienced. If they would start earlier, they could see a bigger change in their future direction.

It all comes down to time. When people plateau, they don't control the present. They live in their comfort zone and become spectators in their own lives. They aren't the director of their life movie, they are a person watching it at the theater. People that accomplish success do so because they are the cause of their success, not the effect of it.

This coincides with one of my favorite laws of the universe, the Law of Cause and Effect. The Law of Cause and Effect states that for every cause, there's an effect and for every effect, there's a cause. Do you want to be the cause or the effect? You can have a certain effect if you cause it to happen. However, the only way to do this is to control the present time. Being effective and achieving an end result. The only way to achieve an end result is to cause something to happen. To take action. To create an effect. With focus and attention on creating an effect, mountains can be moved. With focus and attention on creating an effect, the course of your life and generations to come can change. With focus and attention on creating an effect, your dreams can come true.

But you must control the present time. You must control your motivation and your willingness to move into action. You must constantly be aware of your time and how you're spending it. The power of now is more important than you may think. What you think and do today will have a direct effect on what happens tomorrow.

Assignment #3

Let's increase your awareness of your present condition. Answer the following questions:

1. Where are you right now? What are your senses telling you about your present condition?

2. What actions are you taking today towards your goals? Are you even taking any action towards them?

3. What thoughts do you have? Are they focused on success or failure? Do you think you can improve your life or not?

4. Do you have a plan for the day? Have you read *The Habit Formula* and crafted a daily 'To Do' List?

5. Are you executing that plan? Are you completing the tasks that you've written down in your daily 'To Do' List?

6. Are you busy or are you productive? Are you focusing most of your resources towards accomplishing your goals or not?

7. Are you being efficient with your time or are you wasting it? Are you maximizing your resources (money, time, and energy) or are you wasting them?

Chapter 4

Where's My Nuts?

The Squirrel Method: Squirrels are very clever animals. They are constantly looking for food and things around their environments to make their homes. Have you ever seen a squirrel hanging upside down from a bird feeder? What about hanging like a daredevil from a telephone wire? They dart back and forth to avoid getting smashed by a car. Squirrels are constantly curious and looking for things to create their survival certainty.

In this chapter we're going to explore different areas in your life that you can find the resources you'll need to create an abundant life and find your nuts. A life full of adventure and vigor. Sounds good, huh? Let's get started.

Let's take another look at resources: (aka your nuts.)

- Time

- Energy

- Money

Time

Living like a king or queen is not all about money. Yes, having enough money to not only cover your living expenses but to do what you want, with who you want can be considered freedom. But having the time to do all the things you want during your life can also be considered freedom.

Have you ever read about a Billionaire that died because they were addicted to drugs or alcohol? You could ask yourself why this guy was so messed up? What problems could they possibly have? They have all the money in the world and yet they weren't happy. These people weren't rich in every aspect of their life. Most of these people weren't first generation Billionaires. They inherited a huge company from their parents when they retired or passed and now it's time for the second generation to take over.

The problem is, this new CEO is directly tied to the company. He or she has no freedom. His life has been spelled out for him without his consent. He has to run the business and handle all the issues that come his way. And you would think to yourself, "Lucky guy, I wish my dad or grandpa would have left me something like that!" And maybe that's true for you. Maybe you would do great in that position and explode the company growth.

But many times than not, these trust-fund babies aren't happy with their lives because they can't control their time. They are shackled to their inheritance. They are tied down to the everyday routines of the business. They don't have their own purpose, they have the purpose of their family. This situation often results in deep depression and feeling like they can't live their own life and can result in drug and alcohol addiction.

Look at the life of Augustus Busch IV. He was the great-great grandson of Adolphus Busch and great-great-great grandson of Eberhard Anheuser who formed the Anheuser-Busch brewery in 1860. Augustus Busch IV had a drinking problem. (go figure, right.) He had numerous run-ins with law enforcement as a younger man and was even involved in two deaths. Yet, he was still an executive in a major world conglomerate. How did this end? An international corporation InBev bought them out and took control of the Anheuser-Busch company that had been in the family's possession since it was bought in 1860.

Augustus Busch IV never had the opportunity to show the world what he could do. His grandfather and father had sold too much of their company shares for Augustus IV to have control of the company. It was a board and its share-holders that had control. What kind of incentive did Augustus IV have to put in his time and effort into the company? Not much. He didn't have to struggle or put his ideas out into the marketplace to see if the market would buy. The infrastructure of his company had already been set up and he was a pawn in the operations of it.

No wonder he wasn't happy. No wonder he squandered his position in the company. No wonder he acted the way he did. It's the freedom and opportunity to create a purpose in his life that he was looking for and other people took those things away from him. No one deserves that. Especially when there's something that you're privileged to due to your family's progress. Things could have gone differently if Augustus IV had control of his time.

Being in control of your time is a very important task. Have you ever been involved with a project, you look up at the clock, and you realize that you've been working for hours and hours and haven't even taken a potty break or eaten a meal? You were so involved with this project that you lost track of time.

Unfortunately we can easily lose track of time for the wrong reasons. We can spend the day doing nothing of significance and find ourselves ready for bed without doing anything to move us towards our goals. That's why a concerted effort needs to be made to form a 'To Do' List every single day and move you towards your targets. That's also why we have calendars. We should have them filled with numerous activities in both our personal and professional lives. When your calendar is full, you're making the effort to not only control your time, but to spend it both efficiently and productively.

Take a look at how you're spending your day. When do you wake up? What do you do first thing in the morning? Do you plan your 'To Do' List? Do you run around aimlessly until it's time to go to work or the first activity of the day? Are you organized? Do you know where your keys are? Do you get a work-out in? Are you listening to some training on the way to work or just music? When you get to work, do you participate in the morning meeting or do you sit back and allow others to control what happens during the meeting? If an appointment cancels or reschedules, do you use that time to follow up with old customers trying to reactivate them or current customers making sure that they don't have any new issues? Or do you use that time to see who's not busy and gab with them for a bit?

What about lunch? Do you spend an hour with coworkers and go to a restaurant or do you pack your lunch and use that time to prospect or train on a new skill set that you're trying to learn? What about the afternoon? Are you keeping track of where your sales are coming from or are you bopping around aimlessly from appointment to appointment? When do you go home? When five o'clock hits? Or do you stay later so that you can keep prospecting and following up with clients so you can push the bar just a little bit more? What happens when you get home? Do you order take-out and plop on the couch and don't move the rest of the night? Or do you make a nutritious meal for your family, clean the house a little, and lock yourself in your office spending some time planning the next day's activities? Do you do any self-improvement? What about sex? Do you initiate sex with your partner, or decide that it's too much effort and will take too long? Do you go to bed early or do you piddle around all night, not getting enough rest to tackle the next day?

These are just some of the questions you must ask yourself during the day. How are you spending your time? Is it this or that? Which choice gives you the results that you're looking to accomplish? There's only one clear decision. It's easy if you ask yourself to make a decision between the two things. It's either do this or do that. One of the choices matters and brings you closer to health, wealth, and your true potential and the other does not. But awareness of the choices is what stops most people. Most of us don't pay attention to how we're spending our time and thus we're not in control of it. That's one thing about time, it continues whether we're paying attention to it or not. It's like money, either you control your money or it controls you. You can either control the way you spend your time with activities that move you towards your goals and dreams, or you don't and you end up with the same mediocre results day after day, year after year. Is that really how you want to spend your life?

Squirrels have an innate sense of time. They don't squander it. They know that they must constantly be looking for food and elements to create shelter so they can survive. We humans are a little more complicated but some of us make things more complicated than it needs to be.

Remember the 'no' word that we talked about previously? We complicate our lives by engaging in too many activities that don't matter and we wonder where all of the time went. We seem to do things for other people instead of taking the time to do things for ourselves. Why is that? I think women are guilty of this more than men. Men are expected to go out in the world and earn money and support their families while women play a secondary role at home. But in modern times, this isn't true. There are more women graduating from college and earning higher degrees than men right now. According to a Pew Research Center poll in 2019, 56 percent of college graduates are women. In 2019, for the first time ever, the share of college-educated women in the U.S. workforce passed the share of college-educated men. It's very important that women realize that they need to focus their attention and their actions on themselves first and then take care of others. That's the only way that women can survive and thrive especially when 60% of marriages fail and these women have to float on their own laurels.

Most people's lives are made up of time periods. Their childhood. Their young adulthood. Their parenting years. Their empty nest years. Their retirement years. We all are blessed with the same amount of time during the day. The time periods of our lives may be different, some longer, and some shorter. But we all have the same amount of time to spend today.

An easy way to spend our time as productively and as efficiently as possible is to break up our day into time blocks or time periods. You've got 24 hours during the day. 8 hours ideally is spent sleeping. 8 hours is spent at work. That leaves 8 hours during the day to spend with your family, to maintain your home, and to improve an area of your life. Everyone has chores. Everyone must eat. Everyone has activities to manage. But how much time do those activities take? Remember, you've got an extra eight hours to play with here. Let's say that you spend three hours with your family before it's time for bed. That includes, bathing, feeding, homework, chores, and activities. That leaves you five hours left. Maybe your honey takes up another hour. That leaves four. What can you do with an extra four hours each day? If you said that you could use that extra time to work on your goals, you'd be correct! You've got a precious four hours every day to use it towards accomplishing your goals. You can learn something new. You can clean up and organize your space. You can network. You can finish projects. You can start a second stream of income. You can follow up with past and current customers. You can work out. You can read something useful. You can learn a new language. You can improve a skill set. You can finish your degree. You can write a book. You can remodel a room in your house. There's so many ways that you can use that time productively and wisely.

An effective time management tool is called the Pomodoro technique. The Pomodoro technique divides your time into 25 minute blocks followed by a five minute break. After four 25 minute blocks, you then take a twenty minute break. This focuses your attention to be as productive as you can be in your 25 minute time block as you can without getting burnt out. That's what the breaks are for. It allows you to focus, focus, focus, and then relax for a bit. Then you focus, focus, focus, and then relax a bit. When you can focus your attention on the task at hand, you'll find that you're more productive and efficient at getting things done. You can actually finish a chore. You can actually finish a project because you've got uninterrupted time.

You can use the Pomodoro technique at work too. If you know that you've got follow-up calls to make, you can block out 25 minutes and make as many calls non-stop during that block as you can. You'll find that your numbers will increase because you're not allowing distractions to hinder your progress. Whether it's personally or professionally, you'll find that you can accomplish more during your day if you block out time for each activity and focus your resources towards that activity.

Whether it's working out, finishing a chore, or working towards a financial goal, you'll find that you'll have enough time to do all of it. It's managing time. It's managing your activities during that time frame. It's eliminating wasted time. It's eliminating distractions that rob you of your resources. I've been using this technique both personally and professionally and have been amazed at my own results! There's no excuse that I'm too busy to attend an event or to finish a project or to hit a goal because every day I've blocked out time for all of it and I don't allow anyone or anything to steal my time. If you know how to manage your time and the activities during that time, you'll find that you're never too busy to do anything and everything that you want!

If you're blessed to spend your time the way you want, that's true freedom. If you're not spending your time the way you want, then you must ask yourself how you really want to spend your time. Maybe it's time to multi-task and combine activities. Maybe you want to concentrate on your career but have a passion for writing on the side. Why not combine your career with writing and creating articles and digital products about your career? Maybe you're a marketer by day and a passionate cook by night. If you love to cook and have a really great salsa recipe, why not combine your marketing skills with your cooking skills and have a side hustle of your own jarred salsa that you can bring to the market and sell? There's nothing that says you can only be this way or that way. You can only spend your time doing this one thing or that one thing. You can combine things. You can combine your resources to allow you to follow your passions in any way you see fit.

Do you depend on a weekly paycheck? 76% of Americans live paycheck to paycheck. During the week, most of us trade our time for money. We put in 40+ hours of work and get paid for the skills that we possess. Is your time directly tied to your income? Most of us are. You don't have more passive income (income that's not directly tied to your time) than earned income so we must spend our time earning our money. That's where investments and finding more ways to multiply our money (more nuts) helps us break that time-for-money shackle.

Do you run a business? Do you physically have to be in your office or your business would collapse? According to the U.S. Chamber of Commerce, there's over 28 million small businesses in the United States and 22 million of them have no employees. That means that those people have to go to the office and perform their job in order for income to be earned. I'm in the same boat but not entirely. I have a solo general dental practice in Akron, Ohio. I'm the only dentist thus I have to be in the office to produce 80% of the production that comes in for the day. The other 20% is earned through my hygiene department that does cleanings whether I'm there or not. So at least I have some passive income. I also have real estate investments that pay me another 6% in passive income. But 74% of my income still requires me to go to the office and trade my time for my money.

To live *The Squirrel Method*, we must think in abundance. That doesn't mean just financially. That also means time. How can we have abundant time? We can earn more passive income than we earn directly by trading our time for our money. That's one way. We can combine our talents and start a side hustle to earn more money that we can invest and divert to passive income. Another way could be to buy time.

What do I mean *buy time?* Maybe you're a busy executive and do a lot of traveling for business. Who runs your errands? Who picks your kids up from soccer practice? Who cleans your house and does your chores? If you're traveling and working all of the time, either you do those things when you can, you have help from your spouse or relative, or you hire someone to help. That's right! You can buy time by hiring others to help you with non-productive activities.

If you want to earn more money and increase your investments and passive income, you've got to buy time. You've got to spend more time directly tied to income-earning activities. That means someone else can do the chores and pick up the kids. Then you've got your resource of time to work for you.

What if you're a business owner? How can you buy time? You hire more employees. You hire employees that can sell, do secretarial work, do bookkeeping, do the marketing, and do any other activities that aren't directly tied to providing products or services. This frees you up to negotiate deals, follow up with customers, and create new ideas that can flood the marketplace with your name, your products, and your services.

You can hire a personal assistant to help you with the chores, the kids, and the errand running. This frees up time that you can spend scaling and growing your business. You can also hire a virtual assistant from another country that can help with emails, follow up, video making, and ads. You don't have to do it all alone! If you had more time to work on your business, you could scale and make more money for a fraction of the cost of an assistant or employee that could take the busy, non-productive activities off your plate.

That's what bigger corporations do. They have departments that handle certain aspects of the business. From marketing and advertising to accounting and contracts. The only difference between you and them is the need for their products and services. They have a greater need, thus have a greater revenue stream than you, making it easy for them to hire employees to help in different areas. But you can start scaling your business too by buying time.

The more employees you have, not only are you buying time, you're also multiplying it. How? Because every employee works 40 hours a week. So if you have 10 employees, you have 400 hours worked in and on your business, not just 40 hours if you were a solopreneur. Think about that for a minute. Buying time actually multiplies the amount of work you can get done in your business. That's how people scale their companies. That's how companies grow. They multiply the productivity of their businesses by using the resources produced by their employees, namely their time.

If you hire people to help you with chores and errands, that could save you 10 hours that you can spend on your business. Those ten hours over the course of the year is an extra 13 weeks of work. That's a quarter of a year. What could you accomplish with an extra three months of available time that is free for you to spend on your career or your business? It's amazing how important time can be to your success if you spend it wisely and efficiently.

This is what's fantastic about living *The Squirrel Method*! You know inside what *you're* supposed to be doing. If you want to use your time in a certain way, do it! No one is stopping *you* but *you*. Don't allow outside expectations to influence how you spend your time. You're always in control of your time. Say no if you must.

Hire help if you must. Do whatever you have to do to be able to live with yourself and how you're spending your time and you'll always find happiness, satisfaction, and success. Focus on finding your time nuts!

Energy

Everything is made of energy. The Universe. The Earth. Our bodies. Our thoughts. We need to use our energy to create the reality that we want to live in. Squirrels don't waste their energy deciding which tree they're going to build their home in. They don't waste energy talking with other squirrels and gossiping about which squirrel did what to whom. Squirrels have one purpose and one purpose only: to survive! They use all of their energy conducting activities in order for them to survive. They gather any nuts that come their way.

According to the research of Dr. Mikel Delgado they then use their energy to sort through the nuts and arrange them into categories. Nuts that are solid and can be stored during the winter for later consumption go into one area while nuts that have defects in them and won't last long go into another area for immediate use. They use their energy to gather their food when their food is available and sort them when it's time to store them.

How are you spending your energy? Similar to your time, you have an exact amount of energy. According to Medical News Today, our body energy is measured in calories. Those calories are in the form of food and drinks that our bodies break down and use for bodily functions including repair, digestion, circulation, and movement.

The United States Government states that the average man needs 2700 kilocalories per day while an average woman needs 2200 kilocalories per day to function. Of course, the daily amount of calories depends on your age and activity level that you maintain. Our bodies also metabolize or break down food and drinks differently. Some of us break down the foods we consume quickly while others break them down more slowly.

Different types of foods contain different amounts of calories. For example, one gram of carbohydrates equals four kilocalories, one gram of protein equals four kilocalories, and one gram of fat contains nine kilocalories. So you can see that optimizing your calorie intake can optimize the amount of energy available for you to use during your daily activities.

Optimization is the key. Eating too many calories per day can increase your storage, turning your body into a reserve dump. You can gain excess weight and feel sluggish all day, every day. Learning how to eat properly is the way to go. This takes a lot of discipline because we all know that there's a lot of junk food and processed items in the marketplace. Convenience does not necessarily equal optimization. The way we use our time can be directly tied to the way we use our energy.

In order for us to optimize our energy, we must focus part of our time during the day on planning our meals. We need a balance of carbohydrates, proteins, and fats in order for us to have the maximum amount of energy our body will need for us to perform the daily tasks that we want to perform in order for us to accomplish our goals.

Let's simplify things a bit and get back to *The Squirrel Method*. They are simple creatures. Remember their main purpose is to survive. For us humans, we must not only survive, but we must thrive. But in order to do that, we must simplify the way we use our energy per day. We need to get rid of our distractions and clutter. That doesn't mean you have to live by yourself and live like a hermit, but you must get rid of activities and people that keep you from surviving and thriving.

Let's discuss clutter, for instance. Think of the amount of junk that's not being used or consumed in your house. Think about the stuff that's sitting in the corner of your closet or your garage, for instance. These are things that you may have needed or used in the past, but are either broken or don't serve a purpose in your life at the moment. Why save these things? Most of us are taught not to waste our money. Most of us are taught to save things because you never know when you might need it. But is that really serving you? Is that really allowing you to optimize your energy output? Is your garage so cluttered that you can't even park your car in it? Is your closet so cluttered that you have to have a storage unit to keep all your extra stuff?

If you rent a storage space, and you're not moving or building a new house, then you've got clutter. It's time to get rid of it. You can do one of two things with that clutter. You can either sell the stuff that can be reused by someone else, or you can donate it. Either way, you are freeing yourself of your clutter and also bringing in money from selling your stuff and also from not renting a storage unit.

You've got to pay attention to how you're spending your money. Where's your money going? Cut down on the frivolous spending and you'll find that the amount of clutter that accumulates in your house will also decrease. If you focus your attention on saving to invest your money, you won't want to buy things that don't help you.

Think of money as energy. We want to have the right amount of energy to survive, right? That means we must accumulate the right amount of energy so that we can spend our life the way we want and not how we're forced to spend it. That's where money and clutter come into play. If we cut down on the spending on frivolous items, we can spend our energy on activities that can accumulate energy to store, in this case, our money.

Clutter can also create chaos in your life. How much time and energy do you spend every day trying to find something? Have you ever lost your keys and can't find them? What about your wallet? Organization also needs to become a daily chore for you to manage the clutter and not use your energy unwisely looking for a lost item. Get organized. Get rid of stuff you're not using. If you haven't used it in the past year, get rid of it. If you end up doing a project that needs that certain item, you can always borrow it from a friend or family member or you can buy another one. But more than likely, you won't use that item any time soon.

Get organized. Find a home for everything needed. Hang stuff up. Put similar things in a box or container and get rid of things that are broken, partly used, or worthless. Don't waste your energy ruffling through things trying to find something. Spend your energy now, getting organized and clean. Then you can focus your energy on thriving and not back tracking.

Another way to use your energy wisely is to cut down on distractions. Remember, we not only want to survive, but we want to thrive. In order to keep improving, we need to focus our attention and energy on improving areas of our life. Our skill sets, our activities, and our mindset requires energy. If we're constantly distracted by people and things in our environment, we can't focus that energy on ourselves and our goals.

Everyone wants more money, right? Everyone wants better health, right? Everyone wants a wonderful relationship and family life, right? In order to have those things, you've got to have enough energy to focus on those things. If other people are asking for your time and energy to help them get what they want, then they're robbing you of the energy you need to improve your life. If you're spending your energy on things that don't improve your life, then you're wasting your energy. We need to stop giving our energy away. We need to stop using our energy for things that don't matter to us. We need to stop using our energy helping other people get what they want and not what we want for ourselves.

Other people are distractions. Activities that don't improve your life directly are distractions. We need to realize that we must use those calories that we provide our bodies daily with the foods we consume towards our own benefits and not those of other things and other people. Being busy doesn't necessarily mean that you're being productive. Networking with other people doesn't necessarily mean that you're creating customers. Yes, there are people and activities that we must do in order to keep our lives on track that aren't necessarily tied directly with productivity. But we need to cut down the daily distractions to a minimum in order for us to maximize our energy consumption.

We need to become laser-focused. Our body moves in the direction of our thoughts. If our attention is on people and activities that get us closer to our goals, then we'll start to see results. If our attention is on people and activities that are only distractions and keep us from moving towards our goals, then we won't see the results that we want. Do you understand what I'm saying here?

It's about the control of energy. We need to control the amount of calories our bodies consume so that we aren't sluggish and overweight. We want our bodies to perform efficiently and effectively. We want our minds to be clear and to focus on our goals that we set both personally and professionally. The energy we have is limited, thus to live the life we want and to live simply and effectively, we must live with minimum distractions. Clutter and waste distract us. People and unproductive activities distract us.

Let's talk about where to focus our attention and energy for a moment. I'm talking about goal setting. You will spend just as much energy pursuing a small goal as you will a big goal. You will spend even more energy if you don't set a goal at all. Setting goals is easy. Quantify or describe the target that you want to hit. That's your end point. Then move backwards from your end point and map out the steps and increments that you'll have to take in order to get you from your starting point to your final destination. I map out exactly how to hit your goals in my book and program, *The Backward Rule: The Ultimate Way to Hit Any Target.* It's the roadmap that I use to create a multi-million dollar business and to make sure I'm using my resources correctly.

It's amazing how many people don't set any goals. How are you going to improve your life if you don't set a measured target? A University of Scranton study claimed that 92% of people fail to hit their targets. Another Harvard study found that only 3% of people that write down their goals even planned out their strategies for hitting their goals. The kicker to the whole study was that this 3% of the group that had a goal and a plan for hitting their goals earned ten times more than the other 97% of the group!

This 3% group made a plan for how they would spend their resources. They focused their time on hitting these certain steps and measured their progress along the way. Without accountability, you'll be wasting your time. Without a clear direction of where you're spending your time, you'll be aimlessly moving. That's why a clearly defined goal and roadmap to hit that goal is of the utmost importance!

Learn to use your energy wisely. Learn to use your energy effectively. Learn how to use your energy to hit your defined goals and to improve any area of your life you want to improve. In order to simplify your life, you've got to give up some stuff. Clutter, distractions, and aimless activities will rob you of the energy you'll need to live the life you want, to hit the goals you want, and to improve the areas of your life. Simplify your life using *The Squirrel Method*. Use your energy only to survive and thrive. If you can cut out the distractions and the people that consume your energy, you'll find that you'll have the energy *you* need to take on the things that you want to spend it on and not what others want you to spend it on. Find your energy nuts!

Money

Earlier we discussed how to earn money and multiply it. But we never discussed where to find money. Where are more money nuts? In this section, we're going to do just that.

Most people don't know that they're surrounded by money. Think of all the physical objects you've bought over the years that are in a closet or garage someone and they're collecting dust. Did you ever think of selling them? You don't have to donate everything you have that you don't use. You can create an ad in Craig's List or use one of the apps like Carousell, LetGo, OfferUp, and Vinted to name a few. You can also have a garage or yard sale and get rid of stuff that you call junk. Then whatever is left over, you can gift or donate.

Selling your unused things can actually put some decent money in your pocket as well as clean up your house! Why trip over all that clutter when you can knock out two birds with one stone? You may not realize all the things that can be sold. Old electronics. Old musical instruments. Old clothing. Collectibles. Kitchen appliances. The list goes on and on.

Most people are afraid to give up things, especially when they may have had an emotional tie to them. This is how the condition of hoarding developed. People tie emotional satisfaction or pleasure by the process of buying things and building up their possessions. They feel safe as they drown in the amount of physical items in their house and by the debt they suffer from purchasing all of those things.

In order to make room for the success you want in your life, you must give up the clutter. By giving up the clutter, you can focus your money on ways that can increase your skill sets and ultimately your wealth. Whether it's $2 or $2000, you can use that money to invest in yourself and your future. Instead of being unable to use your extra carport because of the old motorcycle that's taking up room, now you can use it for other things! And think of how much compounding that extra money can do over the next 20-30 years? What's more important? Having a motorcycle that doesn't work or money that you can use in retirement? The choice is obvious!

It takes a lot of courage to make a change. It takes guts to admit you were wrong for purchasing something that you never used and to then decide to sell it and change your life. Find the courage! Admit that you were wrong in your purchase cycle and move on. When that happens, you'll free your mind (and your wallet) to focus on your future success.

What about looking at your utilities and insurance? Where can you find money there? If you combine your home and car insurance, can you save money? What about having higher deductibles and saving on monthly premiums? You can even pre-purchase utilities and lock in their savings. These savings can add up to hundreds of dollars a year in money that you can again use to invest in yourself and your future!

Is there any way you can combine your numerous loans into one payment? There's a lot of banks and financial institutions that can combine credit cards and student loans into one easy payment. And most of the time the interest rates on those consolidation loans are much lower than the interest rates on the individual debt instruments.

What about taking out a 15 year mortgage instead of a 30 year mortgage? The payments are much higher, but the interest you're saving is tremendous. If you bought a house for $200,000 at 4% over 30 years. The interest would cost you $143,739.38. So the true cost of your house isn't $200,000, it's $200,000 plus the $143,739.38 in interest which equals $343,739.38!!! When it's time to sell your house, do you think it will be worth 1.7 times what you paid for it 30 years ago? Maybe. But more than likely not. So who benefits from this transaction? That's right, the banks. If you can't afford the 10 year or 15 year mortgage price, then you certainly can't afford to waste the 30 years' worth of interest payments on that house either. Buy a house you can afford and avoid supporting the banks' efforts.

What about credit card debt? Creating wealth and prosperity for you doesn't start in the hole, right? You don't see squirrels going to the squirrel stores and buying things on credit cards, huh? For some reason, we use our plastic cards because it's easy and convenient and we don't feel the consequence for our spending until we get in over our heads and we can't pay the debt off. Start using cash to purchase everyday items. Like groceries or clothes. If you budget, I know I said the "B" word. If you budget a certain amount for each item and have that in cash, you will limit yourself on how much you spend on those type items.

You can consolidate those credit cards into one easy payment and try to put an extra weekly payment onto that loan so you can eliminate that debt quickly and easily. Then you can use that extra money for your own improvement or to invest for a later date.

What about using your money to maintain the things you have? Your car needs regular maintenance. Your furnace and air conditioner needs regular maintenance. How about your clothes, coats, and shoes? You can easily fix those things when they wear out or are in need of a new part. You don't necessarily need to buy something new when you can repair it. Think frugality. Prioritize who you're giving your money to. Where are your money nuts going?

What about buying and cooking in bulk? A lot of money can be saved by buying food in bulk, cooking it all at once, and then using a Foodsaver to take out the unwanted air so you can freeze your food. Purchase an extra freezer and freeze premade meals to save you both time and money.

What about investing your money in better brands? Most brands that are more expensive are more expensive for a reason. They are made of better quality parts. They use materials that are more rugged and can stand the wear and tear of use over time. You may have a higher price in the beginning but you will find that you'll spend less money over time because you won't have to replace that item as often.

You can also save money by learning to share things. Is there equipment that you can share with your neighbor? Can you share something with a colleague at work? There are hundreds of companies that rent out equipment so that you don't have to actually purchase those machines. Copy machines, computers, outdoor equipment, even cars can be shared and rented. Why use your money to repair and maintain something that you don't use all of the time? Rent it or share it with someone else and save money over time.

We've talked a lot during this chapter about using your other resources of time and energy wisely. Goal setting. Time blocking. Eliminating distractions. Where else can you find money? You can start by looking around your community. Where's the money flowing? Who has the money? Who has nice cars and big expensive houses? What do those people do for a living? What big companies are in your area? What industry are they in? Who has the money in your company? What skills do they have that you lack? How can you gain those skills so that you can have that position? Money is all around you. You've got to pay attention to it. You've got to find where it is and who has it. Then you've got to align your skills with those that have it.

Remember that squirrels are curious. They're constantly looking for food and items to create a shelter. Act like a squirrel. Be curious about your environment and the people that live in it. Look at your own present situation. Where's an area that lacks the results that you want? Where can you find more money? What areas can you cut spending? What areas do you need to control? How much can you cut? How much can you delegate for survival needs? How much can you save to invest?

The more attention you give to controlling your inflow and outflow of money, the more money you'll have to save and invest for your future. Whether that's on improving your skill sets or in products to multiply your money over time, your money needs your attention.

When you focus on money, you'll also start widening your awareness of your surroundings. You'll start to identify where the money comes from and where it's going and maybe you'll be able to align yourself to the other flows. Moonlighting and starting a side hustle can help to align you with other flows of income.

The money basics of *The Squirrel Method* came from the examples of my grandparents. I was blessed to grow up with both sets of grandparents. But I learned different money strategies from both sets. My maternal grandparents worked for a big corporation that ended up going belly up. All of their retirement money that was saved in that company's pension plan also dried up. They put all of their eggs in one basket and unfortunately, that basket dried up. They had another side hustle business but allowed it to die down once they retired and had no other means of money after that other than social security.

My paternal grandparents were a different story. They owned their own business and were able to sell their business and retire off their savings at 56 years of age. They then lived modestly and traveled around the country to see different states and meet people from all different walks of life. Instead of resting on their laurels, they used their money from their sold business to purchase houses in cash that needed remodeling. They then flipped those houses when they were fixed up and took part of their profits to buy more flips and the other part to invest in stocks. When it was all said and done, they had amassed a small fortune that was split between family members.

My interpretation of their living styles was this:

· Live within your means. My paternal grandfather's favorite saying was, "Don't live high on the hog!" That means, don't spend too much money on things that don't matter or won't improve your life in the future.

· Don't put all your money into one basket. Spread your risk and reward over different investment areas so if one dries up, you still have other areas that are going strong.

· Keep working. Even though you're ready to retire from your main career or job, don't allow the money sources to dry up as well. Continue to produce money and invest.

· Invest. Always invest. Learn how to divide your money to live and invest the rest. Then learn how to multiply the investment money for future use.

· Leave a legacy. Success has a roadmap. Work. Save. Live within your means. Invest. Enjoy your life.

· Live your life to its fullest. Don't blame others for your lack. Do as much as you can with the resources you have. Have no regrets. Be smart with your resources and use them to live to your fullest.

Remember that money is energy. The importance we give to money gives it its value. If you can concentrate your time and energy into creating value for other people, they will kindly exchange their money energy for your value add. Remember, the only reason people buy is to solve a problem. If your product or service can solve their problem, they will kindly exchange their money for your solution. You must give yourself opportunities to solve more people's problems by finding more people. By networking. By following up with past customers, current customers, and leads. You've got to follow the money trail.

Where's other people's money nuts? How can you get some? One of my favorite quotes is from Grant Cardone who has amassed almost $2 Billion worth of real estate as of the writing of this book and has a multi-million dollar digital information and sales company. He asks the question, "Who's got my money?" Let's turn that into *The Squirrel Method*. Where's my nuts? Who's got my nuts? Whether it's time, energy, or money, who's got it? Where are they? How do I get some for myself and my family? How do I multiply the nuts that I have? How do I use those nuts wisely? How can I use those nuts to improve my own life and to help me live the life I want and deserve? How can I use those nuts efficiently and effectively?

Start looking at your results at work. If you're in sales, and everyone is in sales, you can calculate the results of your actions. If you see five clients in a day and close two of them on average, that's a 40% closing rate. If you want to earn more nuts, there's a couple of ways for you to achieve this. One is to see more people for presentations. If you can double the number of potential sales, you can double your commission without improving your presentations, your handling of objections, or your closing techniques. Another way to earn more nuts is to increase your closing rate. This requires learning and practicing improved methods for closing sales.

In order to earn more nuts, you've got to increase your level of activity that leads to a sale. Where can you find more nuts? An easy area to look in is in a familiar space: past customers and current customers. How often do you follow-up with people that already know you? Even if it's been years since they've used your services or products, they're still familiar with who you are. There's a gold mine in your backyard that you're ignoring.

Create a follow-up system that keeps you in touch with current and past customers. Use social media, text messages, phone calls, emails, videos, demonstration videos, podcasts, testimonials, personal visits, and small gifts that remind these people that you exist and you're here to help them if they need it.

If your company introduces new products and services, use your current and past customer list as a lead magnet for new business. Let these people know about these new products and services and how they can benefit these potential customers' lives. People buy solutions from people they know and trust. If these people already bought from you before, there's a good chance that they'll buy from you again. Unless you remind them of who you are and what problems you can solve, they will forget about you. Remember that most people live in their own world and are only concerned with themselves. They forget about other people and potential solutions to their problems if they aren't constantly reminded.

That's where marketing comes into play. All the Fortune 500 companies use marketing methods to constantly bombard the general public with their messages, products, and services. They constantly remind people who they are and what problems their products and services can solve. They spend billions of dollars every year on marketing methods that appeal to everyone.

You and I don't have billions of dollars to let people know about our products or services and how they can benefit our customer's lives. But we do have our smartphones that contain customer contact information as well as the capabilities to use technology instruments such as photos, text messages, video, voice mail, and email to keep people informed about us, our products, and our services.

It's amazing how easy it is to find a benefit of your product or service, create a minute video about it, and shoot it out to thousands of potential customers. I do this in my coaching business and in my dental practice. You may think that if you're a white collared executive or doctor, that this method of increasing your money doesn't apply to you. I'd like to tell you that you're completely wrong!

Your customers and patients want to hear from you! People are curious. People educate themselves and do research on products and services on the internet before they make their buying decisions. If you are active on social media and post photos, videos, and articles on the internet, the internet algorithms will reward you with exposure and the ease of discovery. And it's *free*! It won't cost you a dime! But the rewards can be incredible.

Whether you're a newbie, or a seasoned veteran, use the resources you have at your disposal. Constantly remind current and past customers that you exist and you're ready and willing to help them with whatever problem they may have. That's an easy way to increase your money nuts! Find the hidden stash in your own backyard. Follow up techniques can help with that.

Summary

Start paying attention to the details of your nuts. Your nuts are the only resources you have access to. What you do with them dictates the results you are getting. When you change the way you use them, you can change the results you get. When you learn how successful people use theirs, you can emulate them and improve the areas of your life that you want to improve. The roadmap has already been drawn, but most people aren't aware of what it looks like and don't follow the steps to find their final destination.

Wealth, health, and success follows a certain roadmap. Only the people that follow that roadmap succeed. There's certain places to find your nuts. Look in your own backyard first and then build out from there. Can you cut out some spending? Can you sell something that you're not currently using and may be of service to someone else? Can you consolidate debt or increase limits on insurances? What about time? What about energy? Where can you cut and consolidate activities in order to free up your resources so you have them available when you need them for your own purposes and not for the purposes of other people.

There's certain ways to collect your nuts. There's certain ways to spend your nuts. There's certain ways to multiply your nuts. Can you buy time? Can you get help so you're not spending all of your energy on certain activities that aren't directly tied to the increase of resources? If you follow the roadmap written in *The Squirrel Method*, you'll find that you've got plenty of nuts in all shapes and forms to use at your disposal. If you follow the roadmap written in *The Squirrel Method*, you'll find that you'll never waste time, energy, or money because you'll know exactly how to manage and use them effectively and efficiently. Effectiveness and efficiency are the games of the wealthy and successful. To have abundance in all areas of your life, you must focus on using your resources effectively and efficiently. Locate your nuts. Focus on how you're using those nuts and go find more. Remember, who's got your nuts? Then and only then can you get the results that you're after. Then and only then are you simplifying your life and mastering *The Squirrel Method.*

Assignment #4

In this assignment we're going to focus on your resources, how you're spending them, and how you can become more efficient and effective with them.

Time

1. How do you control your time personally? Professionally?

2. Do you create and utilize a 'To Do' List?

3. Do you block out time during your day:

- To work out?

- To work on your goals?

- For family?

- For your friends and significant others?

- For self-improvement?

- For organization?

- For chores?

- To declutter?

- For follow up?

- For prospecting?

- For marketing?

- To create social media content?

- To work on home and work projects?

- To sleep

- To eat

- For sex?

4. Who do you spend your time with?

5. How much time do you spend with people that don't add value or money to your life?

6. Can you multitask? How can you combine things to save some time?

7. Do you trade time for money? Can you decrease the time that you trade for income? How?

8. Can you buy time? How?

Energy

1. Do you control your calorie intake and output? How?

2. Do you know how to optimize your body's metabolism? How?

3. When was the last time you organized your closet? Your garage? Your desk? Your car?

4. Do you have a home or set place for all of your stuff?

5. Do you rent a storage unit?

6. Do you run out of energy by the end of the day?

7. Are you constantly distracted by other people and activities?

8. Is your energy being used to network with people that are directly tied to money?

9. Do you have set goals both personally and professionally?

10. Do you work on these goals every day?

11. Are you measuring your progress towards these goals every day?

Money

1. Do you have a monthly budget?

2. Do you stay on your budget?

3. Do you have a personal financial statement?

4. What can you give up today that you can sell?

5. What can you give up today that can save you money?

6. Where can you find money?

- Consolidate debt?

- Increase deductibles?

- Eliminate payment plans?

- Shorten the terms on your mortgage?

- Repair and maintain equipment?

- Invest in better brands?

- Share or rent equipment and other goods?

7. Who's got your money? Past Customers? Current ones?

8. Where is the money flowing in your community?

Chapter 5

Which Nuts to Choose?

The Squirrel Method: Squirrels make hundreds of decisions every day by instinct. They choose when to cross the road. They choose which nut is good to store and which one must be consumed immediately. They remember where they've stored their stashes when Winter is coming. They find the bird feeder and decide that's a great place for some free food. They constantly decide to act by using their innate instincts. They're very aware of their environment and avoid predators that could be nearby. Their instincts are Mother Nature's way of protecting them and also to give them the ability to survive.

Humans have instincts too, but through experience of life, our decisions can become clouded and difficult. In this chapter we're going to explore how our decisions affect our lives and how to make decisions that will improve the areas of our lives that we wish to improve.

The first area we must concentrate on in making the right decisions in our lives is to simplify the decision-making process. You've got to be black and white on your decision-making skills and get out of the gray zone. The gray zone is no man's land. The gray zone paralyzes you and keeps you from actually taking a side and making a decision. Have you ever been asked a question, to make a decision, but didn't? Maybe you could see both sides of the decision and couldn't make up your mind which way you wanted to go. So what happened? You didn't make a decision at all and nothing happened. That's the gray zone. That's the exact place that you don't want to be. So how do you get out of the gray zone?

To get out of the gray zone, you've got to have the guts to fail and live with the failure. In my eyes, failure is just a lesson. It's just a step that you must take in order for you to get you closer to your goal. Failure is only an obstacle, a thorn in your side. That's all. It doesn't mean *you're* a failure. It means that the decision you made was wrong and it's time to make a different decision. No one that has built a successful life has done it without failing or making a wrong decision at some point during their journey towards their goals. It's part of the journey. How can you learn *what* works until you learn what *doesn't* work?

You've got to be willing to try and see how things work in order to determine if that decision was the right one or not. If it's not the right decision, you've got to be willing to change course quickly and move in a different direction. You can use your past experience to help make your decisions. You can use a mentor that's already been where you are to help direct you in the right course of action. But just because your mentor had success doing certain things a certain way, doesn't mean that what you do will go exactly the same way. Be flexible but be quick to identify when you're off course and learn to pivot.

No matter what happens, don't play the victim blame game. Don't blame your decision failure on someone else. Don't blame your failure on the economy or the government. Take responsibility for the decisions you made and make them quickly. Don't become emotional about your decision either because you won't feel angry, mad, or guilty when you need to pivot and make a different decision. Make a firm decision but don't hold fast to it in case you've got to make a change. Be patient and allow the decision to run its course. Don't be too hasty in changing direction until you know for sure that this particular path is the wrong path to take. Sometimes decisions take time to develop and mature.

Think of the professional baseball player. Most players that are inducted in the Baseball Hall of Fame have a batting average of .300. That means that he averages three hits for every ten times at bat. That's only 30%. If he can hit the ball 30% of the time, he's considered the best of the best! That tells you how difficult it is to be a batter in the MLB! That also tells you that you can fail seven out of ten times and still be considered successful!

Professional forex traders only need to be right 30% of the time too when they can take a 1:3 risk to reward ratio to be profitable. Again only 30%. In life, you could probably be wrong in more cases than you're right and *still* be very successful as long as you can identify when you're on the wrong path and pivot in a different direction.

Another factor in complicating the decision-making process is your beliefs and habitual behaviors. How many times have you believed you should decide a certain way because that's the way you believed you should go? Even though you had never had experience in that certain area, you went with your gut feeling without any basis or proof. This gut feeling is usually your learned belief. But where did this learned belief come from? It wasn't from you. Usually beliefs are formed from our environment. From the people that raised us. From our friends and family. From our inner circle.

If you heard over and over again from a relative that being in debt was bad, your decision to borrow money to improve some equipment in your business that could open up more marketplace opportunities may be stifled. Your belief to borrow money would hinder your decision to expand because you grew up with the false belief that debt is bad and should be avoided. What that relative didn't understand was that not all debt is equal. Consumption debt, debt that's used for frivolous purchases of material goods absolutely isn't good and should be avoided at all costs. But debt that's used to scale a business or improve an area of it that can jump its market share and its profits isn't the same thing.

Think of the real estate business. Most big companies use real estate debt as leverage to grow their wealth without having to put up all the money to purchase the properties outright. Most real estate tycoons put 30-40% down and borrow the rest of the money from a financial institution at a certain interest rate. They could easily pay 100% of the total value of the property but choose not to. Why? So they can take advantage of the leverage their debt gives them.

Using that debt leverage they are able to free up 60-70% of their money to help maintain that property and to buy another one. Their debt is paid by the renters and they bought the property at a price that incorporates profit into the whole equation. They then can hold the property until it's paid off through the renter's payments and they own it outright and collect *all* of the profits with only 30-40% of the money required to control that property. By the time the property is paid off, they will have multiplied their down payment numerous times and still control the asset.

Money is cheap to borrow nowadays. Even Apple, according to their Q1 2019 estimates disclose that they have $207 Billion in cash but still borrowed $7 Billion to scale their business in the research and development areas. They know that money is cheap to borrow and they want to make sure that they have enough money available to them to use in case the economy goes on a downward turn.

These big companies have the right idea about debt. They use it to expand their businesses and to be able to control assets that bring in profits to them and their shareholders. But if you have the belief that all debt is bad, there's no way that you'll borrow any money to expand or improve your business. You'll remain at the same level that you're currently operating at until you've saved enough money to make you move. And that may never happen because it's a difficult thing to do.

I'm not saying your relative is an idiot, but maybe they didn't own a business. Maybe they didn't know *how* to leverage debt to scale or improve their business. Maybe they didn't know how to grow into other industries. That doesn't mean they were wrong, that just means they never experienced the other side of debt and how to use it properly.

What about looking at your expectations of your outcome? If you believe that the result of your decision should be X and instead you get Y, was your expectation incorrect or was the decision to take that certain path towards that certain outcome incorrect? It could be either. If you were an informed decision maker and you followed the advice from a mentor that had used the same steps to get the expected result in the past but this time it didn't work the same way, then maybe that roadmap is outdated. Maybe the expectation was too high. Maybe more action should have been taken. Or maybe more time should have been allotted to the project.

Maybe you expected a certain outcome but didn't educate yourself on the process of achieving that target and you missed. In that case, your expectations were based on a false belief and miseducation. That's where a mentor's wisdom and experience can help. So expectations can play a key role in decision making and goal achievement.

What role does discipline play in success or failure? If you follow *The Squirrel Method*, you'll realize that squirrels use all of their time and energy finding methods to help increase their chances of survival. A simple definition of discipline is, "To give yourself a command and then follow that command."

If you want to lose weight, you must make a decision first that you're going to lose weight. You must then educate yourself on what steps you must take to change your current situation and lifestyle so that you can become slimmer and healthier. When the education is done, then you've got to take action. You must implement discipline and follow through on the action steps you need to take in order to hit your goal. It's about decision making, education, and implementation. That's what makes the difference between those of us that succeed and those of us that don't.

Commitment follows discipline. You've got to commit to the process in order for the process to change the results you've been getting in your life. If you want to pay off your debt and have financial freedom, you wouldn't constantly be spending your entire paycheck without saving or investing part of it. You wouldn't continue to buy frivolous material objects. You wouldn't work in a job that paid you less than your basic needs would cost. In making good decisions and succeeding in life, there's a certain roadmap that must be followed in order to achieve it.

Good decisions come from proper knowledge on the subject. Proper knowledge on the subject leads to a plan of action. The plan of action leads to implementation of those plans. Those plans then lead to certain expectations. Either the expectations line up with your targets or they don't.

The question you need to ask yourself will be:

Will you do what's necessary to make a good decision?

You've got choices to make. You've got decisions to make. You either want to improve your life and supply your family with wealth and rich experiences or you don't. You can't expect to get different results when you make the same decisions and choices day after day, year after year. That's the definition of insanity. To expect different results while thinking and acting in the same way over and over again.

Jim Rohn, a famous businessman and motivational speaker once said, "If you want to change, you've got to change!" Makes sense, huh? You've got to change the decisions you make and choose different actions in order to improve the areas of your life, your business, and your career.

It takes guts and integrity to change. Even when your environment is negative towards your improvement, you've got to tune it out and focus your resources on choosing wisely. Making decisions that benefit you and your life and not the lives of other people is the only way you're going to take a step in a positive direction. I know that sounds selfish. It is. In order for you to break the mold, you've got to concentrate on the knowledge, planning, and activities necessary to break the mold.

Other people have already done it. You don't necessarily have to reinvent the wheel yourself. That's why hiring a mentor that can help you overcome obstacles and keep you on track towards your targets is so important. It's a shortcut. Think of the time, energy, and money that can be saved when someone else lays out a plan for you to follow. They've already been through the trial and error portion of success. They know what works and what doesn't work. Why go through the same thing when you can skip to the head of the line and keep moving forward.

If you grew up in the 1990's, you're probably familiar with *Cliff's Notes*. *Cliff's Notes* were summary books on famous literature that most of us were required to read and study during high school. *The Tale of Two Cities*, *MacBeth*, and *Beowulf* were some of the popular titles that *Cliff's Notes* helped to explain. *Cliff's Notes* helped many of us pass English Literature classes because they helped explain what was happening in the stories and also some insights of the characters and motives for their actions. It was a God-send for most of us that weren't really interested in English Literature but were required to take it and wanted to get a good grade in it.

Think of your mentor as your personal *Cliff's Notes*. Your mentor can help you navigate through unchartered territory and give you insights and motives for certain thoughts and actions that are needed in order for you to hit the goals you want to hit. But you need a little humility and a little courage to admit that your way isn't working and that you need a change.

So which nuts do you choose? You choose the nuts that can make a positive change in your life. You choose the nuts that are healthy and won't harm your body. You choose the nuts that can be stored for later use. You choose the nuts that can be multiplied. The choices that you make are directly tied to the results that you will experience and choose those nuts that will improve those results. It can be as simple as that. Remember the gray zone, you don't want to live there. You want to make a clear decision this way or that way.

When you become used to making good choices in one area of your life, you'll find that it will become easier to make good decisions in other areas. Most successful people aren't successful in only one area of their life. If they make choices that give them abundant wealth, they usually make good health choices, relationship choices, and family choices. These people are all-around happy and live to their potential. But don't get too caught up in one area and ignore the other areas.

Think of your life like a buffet. You don't want to waste your appetite on only one food when you've got the opportunity to experience many, many different kinds of foods. A little here, a little there until you're full. Life can be the same way. You find something that you love, you're successful in, and then you start concentrating on other areas that you want to be successful in too.

As far as we know, we only go around this planet once. How are you going to spend your time when you're here? Are you going to try to live life to its fullest and make good decisions along the way, accumulating an abundance of nuts along the way, or are you living a deadbeat life, waiting until your body and life functions cease to exist.

It really is your choice. Make sure you choose wisely. Make sure your choices allow you to grow and experience all the wonders of life. Set your intention. Intention means, "An aim or plan." Figure out which direction you want to head, gain the knowledge that's needed to move that plan into action, and then move into action. Without deciding to make a change, nothing will ever change.

Choose the nuts that matter to you. Choose the nuts that can help you live to your potential. Choose the nuts that can help to increase the evolution of your family for generations to come. Go for the big nuts first, then you can fill your life with smaller nuts later on. If you can conquer the big ones first, the other ones will fill in what's missing from your life. Another Jim Rohn saying, one of my favorites, is, "Don't major in minor things."

Wasting your resource nuts on activities and people that won't help you improve your life is a bad choice. That choice won't allow you to grow as a person and improve your life the way you want because you're using all your resources on things that won't make a difference. If you concentrate all of your extra time on coaching your kid's basketball team and keep ignoring the fact that your sales skills stink which could increase your income, pay off your debts, and free up some time to then coach your kids freely, is this a wise thing? Is this the right decision to make?

If you're constantly doing things for your family and friends and ignore your own health and are overweight and tired, is this the right decision to make? You've got to learn to master the big decisions and leave the rest alone. It's okay to not be a superhero. It's okay to say no to someone. Become focused on making good decisions for you and not for everyone else. If you start making decisions that can improve your own life, you'll find that other people's lives can improve too because your resource nuts can multiply and you'll have the wherewithal to help others with those resource nuts.

But if others spend all of the resource nuts that you have before you've had the time to use them and multiply them yourself, then everyone misses out. Everyone loses out on the potential that different decisions can make. It's about control and what your vision is for your life. Your vision is the path you want to take. It's the end goal that you're working towards. Put the blinders on and don't allow outside people and circumstances to interfere with that vision. If you can eliminate the distractions, you can free up your mental capacity to make good decisions and choose wisely.

Assignment #5

1. Do you make decisions easily?

2. Do you make decisions quickly?

3. What distractions are in your life that keep you from making wise decisions?

4. Are you afraid of failure?

5. Are you willing to try something new?

6. Do you blame other people and other things for the results that you're getting?

7. Do you allow other people to influence your decision-making process?

8. Are these people positive or negative?

9. Are you ready to make a change?

10. In what area(s) are you ready to make a change?

11. What knowledge do you need to make that change?

12. What mentor do you need to help speed up the process?

13. Will you do what's necessary to make a good decision?

Chapter 6

Help! All the Nuts Are Gone!

The Squirrel Method: Squirrels only know how to act like squirrels. They're very resourceful. They are constantly on alert to survive and protect themselves, their babies, and their stash of food from predators and other squirrels. They live simply. They concentrate their thoughts and efforts in abundance and prosperity.

They never stop looking for food. They never stop building extra homes. Their instincts tell them that they are surrounded by predators that can destroy or steal their abundance. They trust nothing and are self-reliant. In order to survive, they must constantly be looking for more food, shelter, and safety. They bury their food. They run back and forth in an attempt to elude a chase. They look for more and more ways to gather supplies so they are safe and warm during the winter months. They sort their food to identify that which must be consumed immediately and that which can be saved for later months. They are completely aware of their surroundings and if they aren't, they usually die by getting eaten or get hit by a car. It truly is a matter of life and death.

We can live an abundant life like a squirrel too, but in order to do this, we must first get in *The Squirrel Method* mindset. Look around your house right now. What do you see? Are you surrounded by objects that make you happy and proud? Look at your body. Is it healthy and strong or is it flappy and tired? What about your wallet? Is it full of extra cash to spend how you wish or is it full of credit cards that are maxed out? Do you get up in the morning and can't wait to go to work or do you hit the snooze button four times to avoid starting your day?

Being aware of your mental attitude and your present condition is the starting point to creating the changes that will give you the results that you'd like to have. Let's start by simplifying things in our lives. The most basic things we need in order to survive are nourishment, safety, and shelter. We need to master those areas first. So let's start here first and build *The Squirrel Method* mindset from there.

Nourishment

Nourishment can include food and water for our bodies to use and repair itself, but it can also mean thoughts, ideas, and beliefs for our mind. Let's start with food and water for our bodies first. What's your attitude towards your body? Do you love to work out and eat properly? Do you devote money, time, and energy towards making sure that your body is working at its optimal level? If not, why? Do you not plan your meals and find yourself starving so that you go through the drive-thru to feed your body quickly? Do you hate to cook and depend on restaurants and grocery store items to feed your body?

At some point, proper nutrition will become an important basic need and will require a lot of your resources to make it happen. The younger you start making proper nutrition a priority, the longer your life expectancy will be. And not just that, the more enjoyment and adventure you'll be able to experience if your body is strong and agile. According to the National Institute of Diabetes and Digestive and Kidney Disorders claims that 70% of Americans are overweight. 17% of the U.S. population or 51 million people take some type of diabetic medication due to poor diet and insulin resistance. Another 28 million Americans were diagnosed in 2018 with heart disease according to Heart Line. I could go on and on about the poor health choices that we as Americans make. One of the main reasons that we are so unhealthy is that we don't use our resources to make good nourishment decisions.

Yes, it costs a little more money to buy organic produce. Yes, it takes more time to cook a nutritious meal in your own kitchen. Yes, it takes more energy to plan your meals and shop for the right ingredients. But isn't your body worth it? Isn't your family's bodies worth it? If you don't care about yours, your children won't see the importance of taking care of theirs either and all you're doing is passing on poor-decision making to future generations. Is that what you truly want? You're setting your children and grandchildren up to live their lives in an unhealthy way that could make them suffer long term from health issues.

If the government can't bring down medical costs for the country, we the people certainly can, by making wiser dietary decisions. If we don't get sick from avoidable illnesses, then we need to be taking all of this expensive medicine or be constantly needing medical attention. Our bodies can then function and repair themselves the way they were meant to and our resources could be used for other things.

It all starts with what you choose to put in your body. It all starts with how you choose to move your body, or not. It all starts with your choices today. You can change the way your body works and functions with a simple decision you make today. Choose to get some exercise today. Choose to make a healthy meal. Choose to spend some extra time on the internet to find a recipe that's nutritious and tasty. These are simple choices to make, but do you have the guts to make them? You may get some negative feedback from your family who is used to eating junk food. You may get some negative feedback from your spouse because you're spending a little bit more at the grocery store. The question is, are you up for the challenge? Are you sick and tired of being tired all of the time and you're looking around at your family and noticing that they're allowing their bodies to operate inefficiently too?

Make the decision that you and your family are worth it and start making better decisions that can lead to more choices of fun and adventure down the road. Make the decision that you and your family want to take control of how they feel and act. Make the decision that convenience isn't the way you want to live any more. Make the decision that intentional eating for health is the way that you and your family want to go. It really is a simple decision when you think about the consequences you'll suffer or are already suffering from when you make a bad nutritional decision.

You know by your instincts what to eat. It's the famous "Knowing-Doing Gap" that puts a thorn in your intentions. You innately know that a balanced diet will optimize your body's function but yet there's a gap that needs to be filled between what you know innately and what you do. Simplify your life. Get back to basics. When you master this basic principle, you'll see your life and that of your family's change in ways that you never imagined before.

Let's shift gears and talk about our mind nourishment for a few minutes. I'm currently reading a book by Dr. Joe Dispenza called *Breaking the Habit of Being Yourself: How to Lose Your Mind and Create a New One*. In it, he talks about how if you think in a new way, you develop new nerve cell connections and the brain functions in a different way. The brain then creates different chemical signals that are released throughout the body. Those chemical signals are used by the body to move in a different way which causes it to experience different things. This creates new emotions and memories are created from the new experiences that you've just created. This creates a new you all from thinking a different thought or allowing a new idea to move you into action.

This whole metaphysics subject is a fascinating thing. We are now able to study how our minds work and can trace the neurological pathways that successful thoughts take to become successful actions. It was always believed that people never can change, but science is proving that opinion to be wrong. Most people don't change because they think and act in the same ways, thus getting the same results. See, there's no change because the mind is functioning in the same way as in the past and never improves or does something different. If you change the way you think, you can ultimately change the way you act which then gives you different results.

What's your viewpoint on your life? On success? About being wealthy? The importance of your health? On having great relationships? How important is it to you to have community involvement? Do you place importance and value on those things? Have you ever thought of these things before?

You don't have to be considered *deep* in order to take a look at your life and your surroundings and really look at how you think and feel about your life and the world you live in. What you believe and how you look at things are directly tied to the results you're getting in your life. People really can change their minds. People really can change their lives. It's a matter of being aware of the thoughts, ideas, beliefs, and actions that aren't working for you and making a change in those areas.

Your beliefs and your actions create your attitude towards life in general. *The Squirrel Method* drills down to your core beliefs and actions and looks to simplify them so that you're thinking positively and are always looking for solutions to the problems. You'll find that most solutions are secretly hidden in the problems themselves. For example: have you ever started a project and were interrupted by your child wanting something from you. You had to stop what you're doing, take care of your child's needs, and then tried to restart your project but you were out of the flow and couldn't continue. Instead of getting mad or upset with your child or your situation, you could come up with a solution to the problem. The problem is that you have a project to do. The other problem is that you have a child who also has their own project to do. The solution to your problem is to either do your project at a time that won't be interrupted by your child or have your spouse help you with your child and make them in charge of your child's needs for a certain amount of time until your project is completed.

It sounds simple and it is. But it takes planning and your innate ability to identify a potential problem from your child. If you've been a parent for more than a minute, you will know for a fact that your child will need something from you. With a little planning, you can avoid the interruption so that you can concentrate on what it is you're trying to accomplish. The solution is part of the problem. Simplify and break down the problem and you'll find the easy solution to it.

Nourishing your mindset can start with simplifying problems and finding solutions to those problems. When obstacles are broken through, your mind can then concentrate on feeding itself and growing. We'll get more into this process later in this chapter, but I wanted to talk a little bit about mind nourishment as a basic need that you must begin to master. Simplify the problem at hand and allow the solution to find itself. By doing this, you'll free up energy and time to learn and create new ways of thinking that can change different areas of your life.

Safety

All members of the animal kingdom, including our friendly squirrels are constantly on the lookout for potential danger. This can include attacks from predators and man made influences like cars. The Universe or God created their eyes and ears to be strategically placed on the sides of their heads so that they can use these senses to a greater extent to ensure their safety in their environment.

We as humans have ears on the sides of our heads too, but our eyes are only on the front of our faces. Because of this positioning, does this mean that God or the Universe meant for us humans to only look ahead of us? Are we meant to hear the things that are going on around us in our environments but are only meant to look ahead into the future? Hmm, interesting, huh?

Basic safety means that you're aware of what's in your immediate environment and have the ability to change your course of action at any moment pending some type of danger. Most people are very aware of their environment and take the necessary precautions to reinforce their safety. But let's not assume anything here. Let's look at *The Squirrel Method* to ensure that safety is simplified and mastered as a basic need.

Safety can not only mean that your body is safe from someone trying to harm you, but it can also mean that you and your family are safe from outside interference and circumstances. Do you have an alarm system in your house so you know that you and your family and your belongings are safe at night or when you're away? Is your house and property properly lit? Do you know any type of self-defense moves to protect yourself against an attack? Do you have a small supply of canned and dry food in your pantry? What about paper products? Do you have a few thousand dollars of cash readily available at any moment? Do you own any weapons? Are you trained to use them? Are you licensed to care for them and do you have them with you at all times? Do you have a safe place in your home that you could go to in case of a natural disaster or storm? Do you have a garden that can help you with a food supply if something were to happen? How about extra water? A generator in case the electricity system is shut down? What about an extra freezer with stored food?

Are your investments diversified in case one sector gets hit? Do you have a retirement plan that you're maxing out every year? What about a living trust, will, and health power of attorney so you can avoid probate and those hard-to-make health decisions that may not go the way you want? Do you have life insurance to help take care of your family in case something happens to you? What about disability insurance in case you don't die, you're disabled, and you need money to live without working your normal job? What about preplanning your funeral so your family can grieve without the hassle? What about liability insurance in case someone falls on your business property and sues you? Do you have enough car and home insurance to cover your belongings at full replacement costs in case of a fire or natural disaster?

Do you have multiple sources of income in case you lose your job or are laid off? Do you have enough savings in the bank to cover a lay off or natural disaster? Do you possess gold and silver? Do you own any fine jewelry? Do you have any fine collectibles or other assets that can be sold? Are there things that you're not using now that can be sold for money? Do you pay for a service that will protect your online information from identity theft? Do you and your family have passports? Do you have physical copies of your birth certificates and social security cards?

If you're self-employed, can your business run without you and still bring in money? Do you have enough employees that can handle the business if one or more of them leave? Do you have money set aside in case you're disabled and can't work for a time period that would allow your business to continue without you? Do you have a small inventory of excess products in case the supply chain dries up?

Having safety for life's challenges and mishaps is something we need to be prepared for. Never depending on one source of anything can help to ensure that we're safe and we can continue to prosper and thrive. Squirrels never have one stash of food or one shelter. They are always building their safety and security by looking for more. They know their survival is directly tied to their abundance and so they are constantly looking to build upon what they found yesterday and the day before. We can use the same thought-process in *The Squirrel Method* to ensure that our lives can continue no matter what obstacles or hurdles get in our way.

Shelter

Not only can a shelter protect our material stuff but it can also protect your investment assets. Have you named your beneficiaries for your insurance policies and retirement accounts? Are your assets placed in your living trust? Have you named your living trust as the beneficiary of your insurance policies?

What about your retirement investments? Are they protected from a market downturn or recession? Can you direct your investments and place them into investments that have guaranteed growth and protection? Are they in conservative vehicles? Do you have other financial investments set up as a health savings account (HSA) that can help with health costs and also allow for investment opportunities to grow your accounts? What about a personal Roth IRA that can also supplement your company's 401k plan? Do you max out the amount that you can contribute to these accounts every year?

What about taxes? If you own a small business, is your company incorporated? Are you taking every deduction available to decrease your tax obligation? Does your company own your vehicle, pre-purchase supplies or rent, or have any investments that can be used to lower your taxes? Is there a plan on how to sell your business in case anything were to happen to you?

Have you made a household monthly budget plan? What about a personal financial statement? Those plans can identify the holes that appear in your financial shelters. What are your assets? What are your liabilities? How much money do you allocate for basic needs, savings and investments, and fun? What areas need your attention? What areas need professional advice from financial advisors and insurance agents?

What about debt? Can you consolidate your loans into one payment? Can you increase your deductibles on your insurance plans so that you can save on the yearly premium amounts? What about your credit score? Is it excellent? How can you increase it to a great score that will save you money if you were to borrow from the bank? Is your debt consumer debt or debt that's used to improve and scale your business? Debt that can improve or scale your business can increase your income and asset levels and shelter you from any economic downturn that may occur. Can you renegotiate any of your monthly bills-cable, electricity, or heat? Can you prepay your bills and save any money that can be used elsewhere?

Do you perform necessary maintenance and repairs on your appliances, furnaces, and car? Do you keep your home in good order? Do you organize and declutter your environment on a regular basis? Do you upgrade your home features to add resale value and enjoyment?

Mastering your shelter environment can help protect you and your family from an unforeseen disaster. Life happens, but the successful people are prepared for such obstacles and have the wherewithal to weather any storm. How are you mastering your physical and financial shelters?

Value

Now that we've talked about the basic needs of food, safety, and shelter, we need to pivot back to our mindset and talk about the word value. According to Dictionary.com, the word value means, "The importance, worth, or usefulness of something. The worth of something compared to the price paid or asked for it. A person's principles or standards of behavior; one's judgment of what is important in life."

Value thus is a big word! Throughout the course of this book, we've identified one main theme, to live an abundant, successful life, you must simplify things and identify what's important to you. In other words, what has value. Earlier in this chapter we discussed some basic issues that surround our basic needs of food, safety, and shelter. People that live the lives that they want, place a great value or importance on mastering the issues surrounding their basic needs. They find that minimizing their tax obligations is important. They value the need for proper nutrition. They prioritize the way they spend their resources. They make plans and create target goals to focus their resources in achieving.

They plan for the future and protect all that they have created. They major in major things rather than majoring in minor things that don't matter and won't create a rich life for them and their loved ones. In other words, they understand and value The Law of Rhythm. The Law of Rhythm states that all things move in rhythm or cycles. Seasons, tidal cycles, moon phases, farming, and even businesses are all examples. Squirrels know that Winter is on its way by the change in temperatures and kick their search for food and their building of shelters in high gear. They plan for what's coming; cold temperatures and scarcity of food.

People that live a rich and abundant life also plan for the different cycles. They know that they won't live forever. They know that something could happen to them, stopping them from raising and protecting their families. They recognize opportunities in the marketplace and position themselves and their companies to seize those opportunities when they become available. They understand the value of a dollar and have learned different vehicles available to not only shelter their investments but to multiply them using time and the compounding effect.

They understand economic cycles and position themselves and their businesses in order to grow during any cycle. They guard their resources and use them effectively and efficiently. They value their networks and their relationships. They understand the importance of goals, mentors, and plan formation.

They are aware of their successful habitual thoughts and actions and are quick to change the ones that aren't giving them the results they want. They're not afraid of failing and pay attention to the methods that work and wash and repeat the processes. They ignore the distractions that take away their growth. They simplify. They visualize what they want and they create their vision.

What's important to you? What do you value? What should be important to you that you're not paying attention to? What areas of your life should you put more value on? What areas will make a difference in your performance and your results?

Spending Habits

There's only one reason people buy things and that reason is to solve a problem. What we must do in order to inhibit our frivolous spending habits is to prioritize what we spend our money on. Will this item or service enhance our life? Is it of quality and will it last for years of enjoyment and use? Does it really solve a problem that you're having? Does it solve a basic need that's not being fulfilled? Will it get you closer to achieving a goal that you've set? Is it a need or a want? Do you really have the money to spend on this item or service? Are you fulfilling your other financial obligations? Will this purchase put you further in debt?

Our spending habits can be directly tied to the value we place on our status in society. How important is it for you to dress in trendy clothes? How important is it for you to live in a certain neighborhood and drive a certain car? How important is education to you and your family? Do you care to spend extra to eat healthy and organic?

Unfortunately we're also influenced by big companies and their marketing efforts. Big companies spend billions of dollars every year to influence your buying decisions by creating urgency and desire to purchase their products and services. They use psychological warfare techniques such as limited sales, buy one get one free, and new and improved tactics to make you buy what they have.

According to PPC Direct, in 2020, we will see an average of 8,000 forms of advertisements a day. Social media sponsored posts and videos. Commercials on TV and radio. Print ads. Sponsorships. Business signs. Billboards. Podcasts. Presentations and demonstrations. Reviews. Comments and feedback. Likes. Followers. Subscribers. All of which pull on your emotions and try to convince you to buy from them.

The invention of the internet has thrown us into the Information Age. The problem is that it's saturated with too much information. Many consumers use the internet to read reviews and watch demonstration videos before making a purchase. Sometimes the result of this investigation is what I call, analysis paralysis. We've become worried that we will make a wrong decision, that we end up reviewing too much information and never make any decision. So things don't get done. Issues don't get resolved. Or we use and abuse the service people that are just trying to help us solve our problems.

It's become a vicious cycle of problems, internet investigation, and possible sale. In order to live *The Squirrel Method*, we again must simplify the buying process. What's the problem? Is it immediate? What's your budget for solving this problem? Who or what can solve that problem? Is the value of what you will be receiving from that company more valuable than the money you'll be giving to that company?

That's it. That's what the whole buying process is in a nutshell- pun not intended! Keep it simple. Limit your internet investigation to three choices or three companies. Set a deadline for this investigation. You don't want to be spending six months looking at three roofing companies. Most internet investigations can be completed in a few days. Compare their offers and what they include. Try to buy local when you can to help support your community. Request a demonstration and three referrals from actual clients. Then call those referrals and ask them about their experience with this company and whether they solved the problem they had. Choose the product or service that best fits your needs and buy it. Make your decision and act quickly to avoid backtracking or creating doubt in your decision. Ignore outside marketing influences and go with the product or service that solves the issue that you have.

Poor Beliefs

We've got to circle back around to our beliefs and mindset. If you believe in scarcity and that all the nuts are gone, then you'll always live your life that way. You'll save and you won't invest in yourself, your skills, or your potential. You'll be too scared to make a move in your business or your company. You'll be risk averse. You'll stay in your comfort zone and you won't grow. You'll always settle for your current situation as fact and you'll feel helplessness to create change. FEAR (False Evidence Appearing Real) will inhibit your growth and you'll find that your results remain stagnant year after year.

Discouragement or lack of support from those around you will become an obstacle for your success. Others will encourage you to "play it safe" to stay where you are because of "job security." To "not think so big" and to limit your ambition and be grateful for what you have.

All of these beliefs are beliefs of the poor. All of these beliefs form a barrier to your growth and your success. The only limitation you have in life comes from within you. Only *you* can start or stop the success you have. Only you can lose weight. Only you can get better at your follow-up skills. Only you can become organized. Only you can educate yourself about investing and proper money management. Only you can demonstrate your potential. Only you can live the life of your dreams.

It all starts and stops with you.

Negativity. Limitations. Complacency. Appreciation of where you're at now, rather than where you want to go are all beliefs of the poor. They believe that their past and current situation defines their future. They ignore different ideas. They listen to people that demonstrate the same life situations. "Misery loves misery," right? It takes just as much energy to be negative as it does to be positive but the achieved outcomes are very different. One of my favorite quotes comes from Henry Ford who said, "If you think you can or can't, you're right!" If you're a pessimist, and there's a lot of those around, and you think success and prosperity are not for you, guess what? You're right! They're not for you! You won't have the right mindset to work around obstacles when they get in the middle of your path. You won't use your resources effectively towards achieving the goals you've set for your life. You won't make any changes in your life thus you won't see any changes in your life happen. It's a direct correlation with the thoughts that you're thinking and the results that you get.

Fight through the negativity and the resentment that you will find along the way. Most people become complacent and jealous after life hits them in the face a few times and they give up. Don't be like the masses of people who are happy with being average. Being average is for losers and quitters. Being average is for those people that have given up, who have settled for their comfort zone and have quit on their goals and their dreams.

We always encourage our children to dream and to use their imaginations, but as we get older, we lose those inspirations because we are expected to be responsible and practical. You can still be responsible and practical as you're going for your goals. You can still be responsible and practical as you improve your finances, your health, and your mindset. Isn't being an example the best teacher for your children? If you're constantly improving and moving out of your comfort zone, your children will learn the same habits and can inspire greatness throughout their lives.

It takes commitment and persistence to keep moving the bar on your success. Why be poor when you could be rich? And I don't mean just wealth. I mean health, mindset and attitude, and your relationships. Why not have it all? It's possible and there's millions of people on this planet that have it.

So why not you?

Why can't you break the cycle of poverty, of poor health, or bad relationships? Why can't it be you that earns a lot of money and has the mindset of saving to invest? Why can't it be you that finds love and surrounds yourself with it every day of your life? Why can't you travel and enjoy all that life has to offer? Why can't you be fit and healthy and celebrate life's adventures? The possibilities are endless if you open your mind to them. You've got to get rid of the poor beliefs and open up to the vast possibilities of success in any area of your choosing. Our mindset and what we believe in forms the course of action our bodies take which in turn gives us the results we achieve.

Assignment #6

Body Nourishment

1. Are you eating properly?

2. Are you feeding your family with nutritious, vitamin-dense foods?

3. Do you cook?

4. Do you know what foods to consume to maximize your body's performance?

5. Do you exercise at least three times a week?

6. Do you have health concerns?

7. Are you under the care of a physician?

8. Do you know how to have a healthy and fit body?

9. Are you willing to do what's necessary to have a healthy and fit body?

Mind Nourishment

1. What's your viewpoint on your life?

2. What do you think about being successful or people that are successful?

3. What's your opinion about wealth and wealthy people?

4. Do you think it's important in having great relationships?

5. How important is it to you to have community involvement?

Safety

1. Is your house properly lit? Does it have an alarm system?

2. Do you have a stash of canned/dry food and water?

3. Do you have a stash of cash just in case?

4. Do you have any weapons?

5. Do you have a safe place in your house in case of an emergency?

6. Do you have an extra freezer?

7. Do you have a generator?

8. Do you have some self-defense training?

9. Do you have a retirement account?

10. Is it maxed out and diversified?

11. Do you have a living trust, will, and health power of attorney?

12. Are your assets properly placed in your living trust and will?

13. Do you have life, liability, and disability insurance?

14. Do you have multiple sources of income? How many?

Shelter

1. Are your retirement investments protected in case of a market pullback?

2. Do you have a health savings account?

3. If you own a business, do you take advantage of every tax deduction available to you?

4. Do you have a planned monthly household budget?

5. Do you have a personal financial statement?

6. Do you have debt? Can you consolidate them into one loan?

7. Do you keep up with frequent repairs and maintenance when needed on your house, car, and appliances?

8. Are you organized?

Chapter 7

Live by *The Squirrel Method*

This entire book brought a serious topic and filled it with humorous antidotes. My entire intention was to make you look at the way you live your life and compare it to a simple creature like a squirrel. Obviously, our lives are a little more complicated than a squirrel's, but the lessons you can take away from studying their lives and how they and other members of the animal kingdom survive in their environment can translate into your life and help you improve any area that you want to improve.

The Squirrel Method is a culmination of all of the knowledge and experience that I've had so far in my life. I've studied hundreds of successful people. Athletes. Tycoons. Celebrities. Philosophers. Religious icons. And I can tell you one thing that they all have in common, they all are laser focused on their own nuts and use their resources they have to accumulate more! They're selfish in their ambition and their dreams and at the same time, they're the most generous people on the planet, solving problems for the masses of people that live on the planet too. So you truly can have it all. You can really do everything and anything that you want in life as long as you make good choices and don't harm others at the same time.

Start by focusing your resources inward and then you can spread them to others outward. Our ideas are like tiny seeds that if nourished and allowed to grow, can change the way people conduct their lives. One small idea can become a massive product or service. One small idea can translate to any language and cross any border. One small idea can make a big difference if you allow it to. If you allow that tiny little idea to flourish and grow together we could solve the world's biggest problems like poverty, hunger, and war.

Let's tie in *The Squirrel Method* analogies and get you set to explore your potential.

During this entire book, I talk a lot about money and finances. Money is an important subject in everyone's life. Some people have it. Some people don't. Some people want more of it. Some people hate it. Some people base their life on it. One thing that money can't do, is to make you happy. One thing that money *can* do is to give you the freedom of choice. Who doesn't want freedom of choice? Money's important when it can be used and circulated. It can buy security. It can buy shelter. It can buy food.

Money can give you the freedom to choose how you spend your resources and with whom. Money can buy knowledge. Money can buy experience. Money can allow you to travel and experience adventure. Money is energy. If you open your mind and change the way you think about money and how to make it, save it, and multiply it, money can pass through you and directly into your bank accounts. Wouldn't that be wonderful? To have direct access to a money pipeline that spews out money, all for you. All for you to direct. All for you to tell it what to do.

By using the strategies in *The Squirrel Method*, you can tap into the money energy and start to direct it to flow to you and your family. But one thing you've got to do with that energy is to pay attention to it. Money gravitates to ease. Money goes where it's wanted and appreciated. If you hate money. If you don't pay attention to money. If you don't make money an important part of your life, money will go elsewhere. Money will find the people who want it. Money will find the people who pay attention to it and use it. Money will find the people that appreciate it and align themselves and their mindsets to accumulate more of it.

You don't have to be a billionaire. You don't have to own a Lamborghini. You don't have to own a Fortune 500 company to be wealthy. Being the top dog may not be for you. Being a CEO or a top level executive may not be for you. That's okay. You don't have to be in these top level positions to be rich and lead a wealthy life. But for some people, it will mean taking on the responsibility that goes along with these types of career roles.

Living the money principles of *The Squirrel Method* means that you never stop trying to tap into the money energy pipeline. An easy way to tap into this energy is to start to think differently about money. Think of it as a good thing. Don't be ashamed to have it. Think of it as potential and possibility. Squirrels don't hate their resources. They don't tell themselves, "I'm not allowed to have the nuts from my neighbor's tree, so I'll just stay on this property only." No! Squirrels go as far as they can to accumulate their abundance of resources. Squirrels don't ignore them. Squirrels use every day of their life to explore their environment and accumulate goods to help ensure their survival.

They don't allow other squirrels to talk them out of their survival or prosperity. They don't tell them that they've worked hard all day collecting nuts and they should think about quitting, getting another job, or taking a vacation. Of course, I don't know how squirrels communicate because I've never talked with one, but as far as I know it, squirrels rely on their God-given instincts to supply abundance and they don't ignore those instincts to survive and thrive.

How are you ignoring your instincts to survive and thrive? Even if you're having a pretty good life so far, you're ignoring at least one area. Maybe it's love and connection with others. You're so busy trying to achieve financial success that by the end of the day, you don't have anyone to share your success with. Maybe you're surrounded with family and love but you haven't really pursued your dream of being a writer or artist. Maybe you're doing well financially but you suffer from migraines because of your diet and stress that won't allow you to relax and have some fun. There's always at least one area of your life that you're ignoring and that's where I want you to look at.

Look around you now? Look outside. Is there an abundance of blue sky? Is there an abundance of trees? Flowers? Air to breathe? Animals? Mother Nature is based on giving everything that lives on this planet, an abundance. There's always plants to eat. There's always air to breathe. There's always water to drink. There's always a beautiful sunrise and sunset every day. Mother Nature supplies us with resources and renews those supplies so there's enough for everyone and everything to enjoy and consume.

What about money? Is there an abundance of money on this planet? There's money everywhere. Look for it. Have you ever driven to a new city and happened to find yourself in an affluent neighborhood? Did you ask yourself what those people did for a living or how they got the money to pay for those houses? I have. I drive through neighborhoods in my own area and bask in the wonderment of the abundance and affluence of money.

The question you must ask yourself is who has it and what do you have to do to get it! But if your mindset is filled with hatred and dislike of money, you'll never open up your mind to the possibility of having it. You won't align your thinking and your actions with that of creating value for people to buy. Remember, people buy things to solve a problem. If you can figure out what problems are more valuable to people than their money, you too will tap into the money pipeline. When you help others find solutions to their problems first, they will help you find solutions to your problems afterwards through the exchange of money.

Mindset has to come first. It must become your primal instinct again to focus your attention on money. You've got to become obsessed with it first so that it knows that you're interested in it and it will begin to listen to your desires of having it in your life. Affirmations and mindset activities are a great way to start to align your energy with that of money. When you align your energy with that of money it makes you feel good.

Affirmations like:

"I always have money."

"I'm so happy that money flows to me through multiple sources in every way."

"I love money and I love how it makes me feel as I use it in this prosperous and abundant world."

"I cherish my relationship with money and find ways of nurturing and growing that relationship."

But the only way you can connect to its pipeline is through your actions. You must start by identifying what skills are necessary in your industry to connect with the pipeline. The top money earners in your company have certain skill sets that allow them to bring value to the marketplace that is connected to the money pipeline. Find out what those skillsets are and go on a mission to get them and become a master at them. By mastering your skills, you can become valuable and irreplaceable in your company. Being valuable and irreplaceable gives you freedom of choice. Being valuable and irreplaceable aligns you with the creative powers of imagination. Through imagination comes innovation. You need that freedom to explore what problems and issues the marketplace has and then have the freedom to develop solutions for them.

If you're a secretary, you won't have the freedom to create. You'll be bogged down with typing, filing, and setting up appointments. Your talents and creativity won't be utilized by your company because you've got common skill sets. Look at your paycheck and that will tell you how common your skill sets are. The more valuable and rare your skill sets become, the more zeros you'll see on your paycheck.

Start connecting with the money pipeline by changing your mindset and your core beliefs about money and your connection with it. If you don't think it will happen for you, it won't. You won't be open to changing your skill sets and your opinions about life and nothing will be different for you. Nothing will change. Nothing will improve.

If you don't believe in personal development and personal growth, the money pipeline will connect to someone that does. Money loves to bring value to someone. Money loves to be important. Money loves to solve problems. If you don't think that you or your skill sets are important enough to help others, then you will never use your resources to improve. And the only way to improve those skillsets is to role play and practice. Test out your new sales skills. See what works and what doesn't work. Build and improve the skills that work until you've become a master at them and they become habitual where you don't have to consciously think about them anymore. Then you can move onto another area of your life that you want to improve. Don't get caught up with changing more than one thing at a time. If you start to change too many things in your life, you can become confused and things can get quite chaotic.

Focus your attention and resources on improving your skills incrementally until you've mastered that level. Then build to the next level and the next level. It's difficult to go from $50,000 to $500,000 but it's easy to go from $50,000 to $60,000 or even $75,000. And then $75,000 to $100,000. Then $100,000 to $150,000 and so on. If you do the math and work backwards from your set target, you'll know where you've got to improve. When you do the math, you'll calculate how efficient and productive you'll need to be every day so that you can hit that goal. Doing the math represents resource energy and is directly tied to money energy. Money is attracted to resource energy when it is pushed to its limits. That means that you're improving and progressing towards your goals. Money loves that. It can sense that there's something different in your activity. It can sense that you're trying to align your energy to connect with its flow.

Next you look for problems to solve. Remember problems are opportunities to connect with people that have money to spend. Most people shy away from problems. Most people shy away from hassles. They do this because they don't have the right beliefs about problems. They don't know that the only reason people buy is to solve their problems. Maybe your product or service can't solve their problems, but if you don't look for them and talk with these people about their problems and actively seek them out, you'll never know and you'll miss the possible connection to a revenue source.

Money is directly tied to positive energy. Problems are made of negative energy. Your job is to connect to the problems and solve them, thus turning the negative energy associated with that problem into positive energy. The problem is solved. The customer is happy. They reward you with money. They reward you even more with future business. They tell all their friends about you and your company. They write positive reviews about how you handled their problem. The positive energy creates a spider-web effect that spreads throughout the community and beyond.

But you've got to tie into that positive energy of money. You've got to direct it where you want it to go. You've got to align your thoughts and resources to it. You've got to love it. You've gotta want it. You've got to assure it that you know what to do with it and that it will be safe in your possession and you'll find ways to multiply it. You've got to give more value to your customer than the value of the money they're parting with.

That's how you accumulate wealth. That's how you build your bag of nuts. That's how you create the freedom of choice that everyone *should* want in their lives. It all starts with your mindset about money and how to connect to its energy.

Another thing to consider is the number one. One is a lonely number and money energy doesn't like this number. One means that you don't have a lot of something. One means that it can be used up and gone forever. One can mean the difference between prosperity and ruin. Even if that one number is a big number, it's still the only one number. It doesn't have friends. It doesn't have associates. It doesn't have any extra support in case something bad happens. One is never a good number to have when it comes to money.

Let's consider one source of income. This book is being written after the Covid shutdown of 2020. Over 40 million Americans were laid off from their jobs because industries and companies were shut down trying to contain the Covid outbreaks that were happening. These people discovered really quickly that one income wasn't enough to sustain their household or their lifestyle. I myself, realized that three incomes wasn't enough since my main income was the one that closed.

Having one main source of income can be a great thing until that one main source of income is shut off. What happens if you're injured or sick and need time to recuperate? What happens if you get laid off or fired? What if your company relocates and you're forced to move or you're forced out of the company? There's so many scenarios that could happen that could cut off your one source of income.

Now let's look at how we can multiply those sources. An article on Wallethacks.com claimed that the average millionaire has at least seven sources of income. That's definitely something to strive for. Some of those income streams include active income (income you earn doing your job or owning a business), investments (from dividends and owning other businesses), real estate (from rental income and appreciation), royalties (from songs, digital products, books, and other copyrighted materials), and licensing (from patents and other agreements). Every time they invest in something, they buy an income stream whether it's a business or a rental building. Each investment buys control over that asset and a percentage of the profit from those assets. They then can use those profits to buy more investments that give them more profits. And the cycle continues over and over again.

Being average means having one source of income that could dry up at any time. People with multiple investments, businesses, rental properties, royalties, and licensing products have income streams that are endless. All of their investments spew off money that can be used and multiplied. They're not dependent on any one means of wealth in any one area or industry. They spread them out over numerous industries. When one industry goes down, they have others that are either rising or holding steady. Like the professional forex traders and baseball players, they keep themselves in the game by spreading out their risks over multiple industries and keep playing the game.

Squirrels don't find one nut and keep it safe. They find hundreds, even thousands of nuts per season, group them together, and hide them for the future. They never know if one batch will go bad, if they'll forget where they hid a batch, or if another squirrel or animal will steal a batch. It doesn't really matter to them because they have an abundance of food. And we as humans need to have the same abundant mentality.

"I'm good. I have all that I want," are familiar sayings of the average person. They have a poor money mindset and it shows in their bank accounts. Money wants to go where it's loved and where it's the star of the show. If you quit on improving your skills and you quit on solving other people's problems, then you've quit on money and money will quit on you. It's a very simple concept that needs to be emphasized. Never depending on one income can be the mindset that can save your butt when a recession hits.

How can you keep a full money pipeline? We just talked about having more than one source of income. Building your skill sets up so that you can have extra money to invest in other income streams is the first step. Where else can you find money?

We talked earlier about solving people's problems. You should be spending a lot of your time looking for people that have problems. Prospecting in your community and your industry globally. Reactivating past clients. If these people bought from you in the past, they are more than likely willing to do business with you again as long as you were nice to them and solved their problems. Remember that people always have problems. Some are new. Some are old. Sometimes they don't have the problem that your product or service could solve in the past, but they have it right now. Unless you communicate and follow-up with these past clients, they will forget you and buy from a competitor and no one wants that!

What about current clients? Are they using your products and services? Do they need more? Do they know someone that they can refer you to that may be a good fit for your products and service. Referrals are an easy way to fill your pipeline with business. The name of the game in business is numbers. The more people that you can communicate with about your products and services, the more people will fill your pipeline with leads and later money.

Using your time efficiently and effectively is another way to keep your money pipeline full. If you can keep your schedule full of potential clients, you'll have a better chance of making a sale and increasing your income. If your calendar is full of potential clients, you have more opportunities to solve more problems. It's about opportunities to connect with the money energy.

You don't see a squirrel hanging out watching TV, do you? They're constantly gathering food and making shelter. They're mastering their basic needs for survival.

Money can provide our basic needs as humans, therefore, we should treat it as the top priority every day. We need to make the effort to keep our calendars full of money connection opportunities.

We waste so much time and energy on activities that don't connect us with our freedom of choice. I was the same way. I would binge watch Netflix series. I would go out and spend entire weekends with my friends hanging out, drinking, and dancing. None of those activities did anything to increase my wealth. None of those activities gave me freedom of choice. Yes, I had fun. Yes, I have lots of photos and videos of our adventures, but it didn't move the dial on my wealth or prosperity dial. All it did was waste one of the most valuable resources I had, which is time.

The Squirrel Method demonstrates The Law of Rhythm. The Law of Rhythm states that everything has a cycle. Seasons, business cycles, and economies all go through up and down cycles. When it's fall, squirrels are busy collecting nuts and hiding them so they can use them during the Winter months when it's cold and there's a shortage of available food. They keep their pipeline full by storing excess food.

If you know that your business cycle follows the holiday season, then you know even in November and December, you'll be prospecting, marketing, and doing follow-up to keep the income opportunities plentiful when the holidays are over. You're planning for the winter by giving yourself opportunities in the spring and summer when the buyers are plentiful.

All of this talk ties into you living your purpose. What is your purpose? What talents do you have that you can share with the world? When you make your fortune, how are you going to spend it? How will you help your family, friends, and community? What types of relationships do you want in your life? What does your ideal body look like? How do you feel in this ideal body?

Having the freedom to choose who you want to spend your time with and what you do with your time means wealth. But in order to have that freedom, you've got to pay close attention to the money energy. If you don't, the results that you're experiencing every year won't improve. As money's value decreases (called inflation) you'll find that money doesn't go as far as it used to in your life and you'll focus your attention on your lack of money instead of the opportunities for more.

Everyone should be self-sufficient. You don't see squirrels standing in line for their government check. They know that Mother Nature will provide an abundance of their basic needs and their job in life is to accumulate that abundance and use it to survive.

We're no different than the animal kingdom, but somewhere we lost our way. Somewhere we started to believe that average was okay. That our comfort zone and making just enough money to get buy was the lifestyle we should adopt. That the American dream of 2 kids, a house, a dog, and a white picket fence would protect us from life's crazy twists and turns.

What we didn't realize is that only money and prosperity would protect us from life's crazy twists and turns. Only money would give us the freedom of choice that is an essential part of the American dream. Somewhere along the way we felt entitled to the American dream instead of working hard for it. Why is working hard so taboo in today's society?

Why is going out on your own and starting a business that you can directly control your money pipeline too hard to fathom? Why do so many people spend their hard earned money on frivolous material goods and don't spend it on assets that can spew off even more money for them to direct and enjoy? Somewhere along the line, the importance of money and connecting to it and its energy was lost. Somewhere along the line, money wasn't the most important tool to use for freedom. And it's a shame. It's a shame that we haven't been able to use our creativity and imagination to connect with the money energy and solve the world's biggest problems of poverty, hunger, and war. I'm hopeful that the simple philosophies in *The Squirrel Method* can wake you up and open your mind again to the possibility of wealth and prosperity. To the possibility that you can make a difference in your family, your community, and the world. It only takes one idea to make a difference but if you're not looking for it, it will be lost forever and no one gains.

And what about our basic needs of food, safety, and shelter? If you can't prosper in *those* three areas, what do you think your life looks like? Do you think you'll be relaxed and at ease? No! You'll be desperate. You'll be angry and resentful. You'll be stressed out trying to find a way to provide the basics to you and your family. Or if you're really lacking in those three areas, you'll be complacent. You'll have the mindset that wealth and prosperity is for other people and that you're happy living on the street and in poverty because that's the cards that you were dealt in life.

There's hundreds of millions of people on this planet that feel complacent and feel that it's other people that can have freedom of choice. That they can't make a difference. That what they do or say doesn't matter. They beg. They steal. They act violently and hurt other people. All because they don't believe in themselves or their abilities to be valuable to their communities and connect to money. They don't believe that anything is possible for them and they act accordingly. And the people that do believe that their ideas and skills matter are the ones that connect with money and ultimately support those that don't.

Money can't buy happiness but it sure can buy enough of your basic needs to feel rich. It can help protect your family from incidence. It can buy income streams that can allow your wealth to multiply. It can boost your confidence to look for more of it. It can change your family's trajectory in the future. It can help other people solve their problems. It can ultimately give you freedom of choice. And that's what we've been talking about throughout this book.

Summary

Living by *The Squirrel Method* is not some hocus pocus ra-ra stuff. It means living your life to its fullest. It means that you're not only mastering the simple basic needs that you and your family have but you're also kicking ass and taking names! It means that you don't settle for all of the mainstream media's negativity and politically-charged rhetoric. You're smarter than that. Living by *The Squirrel Method* means that you don't allow outside influences to take control of your own economy. It means that you're aware that there's opportunities in your environment and beyond to connect you with the money pipeline.

Living by *The Squirrel Method* means that you're positive and hopeful every day that someone or something will come into your life and teach you something that you can take your life to the next level. You understand that life is not about money, but that money is an important component of life that can mean not only survival but the ability to thrive and lead a rich and meaningful life.

Living by *The squirrel Method* means not only a life of achievement but also fulfillment. One who practices t methodology knows how thoughts directly affect actions and results. One who practices this methodology chooses to be a lifelong learner, not afraid to be wrong and not afraid of failing as an integral process of learning and improvement.

Living by *The Squirrel Method* gives you purpose to direct your life down a certain course. It helps with direction. Ones who practice this methodology realize that they too can make a difference in their family's health, wealth, and prosperity, but also that of their communities. This person constantly nurtures their ideas and finds ways to bring them to the marketplace to help solve other people's problems.

Living by this methodology means that you never settle for just one thing. One income. One friend. One kind gesture. One idea. They know that the world is full of abundance and just because they get their share, that there's plenty of wealth and abundance for everyone else. They don't feel bad that they are achieving their dreams and their neighbor is not. They instead, help their neighbor look for opportunities to improve their lives.

This methodology is truly encompassing. I am living proof that you can have it all. You can live an abundant life no matter where you grew up, how much money you started with, and who your family and friends were. It all starts with your mindset and whether you believe that you can improve your current situation no matter what it looks like. It all depends if you think you can do it or not because only you can do the work that's necessary to achieve your goals. Only you will have the willpower and persistence to keep going when obstacles and setbacks happen that want to stifle your progress. Only you can pay the price necessary for success in any area of your life.

No one can take away your progress using *The Squirrel Method* if you've done it correctly and tapped into the abundant way of thinking. If something goes wrong and you miss a deal or an opportunity, you know that the next one is already waiting for you to pursue because you've already looked for it and have it waiting for you to complete.

We humans have an advantage over squirrels that can be exploited by this methodology. We have intellectual faculties like reasoning and imagination that squirrels don't possess, at least that we know of. We have the ability to nurture an idea and birth it into reality. Think of the smartphone or tablet that you're probably reading this book from. Think of the crazy thoughts that Steve Jobs had in his mind when he thought that everyone wants to be unplugged and have the freedom of connection to anyone and any information in the world at the touch of their fingertips. Those are some crazy but powerful thoughts. I'm sure there were a lot of people that thought he had gone mad when he was planning and designing these products with his engineers. But we're so glad that he did it! Think of how boring and difficult our lives were before the internet, before the telephone, before modern transportation.

All of these ideas came from one person that wanted to solve a problem. Then they got other people onboard their idea train to create physical products that people could use. That's ingenuity. That's progress. That's bringing *The Squirrel Method* to life. Seeking opportunities and finding ways to make things happen. These pioneers of industry and technology didn't sit back on their laurels, they kept pursuing and improving their products and services until they died. I always think of what our lives would be like if Steve Jobs would have lived another 30 years. What other crazy products and services would he have developed and brought to the market for all to enjoy.

But you and I aren't as talented or smart as these tycoons of industry and technology. That's okay. *The Squirrel Method* can be used by anyone that wants to improve their lives and live them to their fullest. This methodology was meant for anyone that wants to improve their lives and not only survive but thrive.

People who live by *The Squirrel Method* believe that their resources of time, energy, and money are precious and that they must use these resources wisely. They push. They shove. They manage their activities during their day so that they can get the most out of the time that they have. They don't waste their resources. They use them and they multiply them. They buy time through using employees' resources and by allowing other people to complete tasks that aren't directly tied to the money pipeline. They don't just want to be busy, they want to be productive. Remember there's a difference. Anyone can look busy, but people that are productive move the dial in their life and that of their company's.

Those living by *The Squirrel Method* take responsibility for their lives and the outcomes that happen. They are always striving for improvement in all areas. They don't settle for bad health. They don't settle for minimum wages. They don't settle for anything average or mediocre. They want more. More money. More friends. More ideas. More opportunities. More knowledge. More mentors. Better daily habits. Better health.

Living by *The Squirrel Method* makes you aware of the basic pain versus pleasure principle. While your friends and family do everything to avoid pain and problems, this methodology pushes you through the pain so that you can find pleasure from your efforts. When most people think that problems are bad, you've learned to seek problems from others because problems are opportunities to connect with the money pipeline. When you've made that connection, then you can help others with your products and services. This in turn creates a money flow directly into your bank account which then can be used for family adventures and for fun.

The Squirrel Method can become confusing if you're trying to improve multiple areas of your life at once. It's not meant to be this way. An easy place to start is with your attitude. If your attitude is that of the average person, that improving your life isn't meant for you and your situation, then this is exactly where you must start in order to start the improvement journey. Then you need a reason why you want to improve. If your reason why is not strong enough, you will quit your improvement journey at some point down the line when things start to become hard and complicated. Your reason why is your motivation and fuel to be able to get around and through any obstacle that may get in your way during your improvement journey.

And trust me, there will be many, many obstacles along your way. Les Brown, a motivational speaker and former Ohio Representative said, "When life knocks you down, try to land on your back. Because if you can look up, you can get up. Let your reason get you back up."

That's why you've got to have an abundant mindset. You've got to have the improvement mindset. If you fall back on your laurels, another squirrel (life or the economy) can take it from you. It all starts and stops with your mindset. If you think you can't do it, you won't. If you think you can and you keep that mindset, you'll be able to work around anything that gets in your way of making progress. Once you find success in one area of your life then you can move onto other areas using the same methodology. Why have one friend when you can have thousands of friends. They may not all be close friends, but remember the old saying, "Your network is your net worth." It's not only who *you* know, but *who* knows you.

Having fun and being self-sufficient is at the core of *The Squirrel Method*. Being in control of your life's purpose and living that purpose is the driving force of your survival. How do you want to be remembered by your family and friends? Will your community remember you or your products and services? Will anyone even care that you're not around anymore? If you're living by *The Squirrel Method*, you're living to make a difference in your family and your community and you're showing everyone how important it is to everyone that you live your life to its potential!

10 Core Philosophies of *The Squirrel Method*

1. Positive mindset and attitude- anything is possible

2. Abundance is everywhere- there's enough for everyone

3. Look for opportunities- seek problems to solve

4. Love money- money energy flows where it's appreciated

5. Never depend on one of anything- one income, one opportunity, or one friend

6. Continue to learn and improve through mentors and training

7. Master the basics first- nourishment, safety, and shelter

8. Learn how the wealthy earn, save, and multiply their money

9. Get rid of old myths, beliefs, and negativity about wealth and prosperity

10. Use your resources wisely. Learn how to buy them and multiply them to create a surplus that can be shared with others.

About the Author

Stephanie Aldrich is a general dentist, speaker, trainer, entrepreneur, and author of five other books and programs including *There's No Crying in the Man's World: A Woman's Guide to Succeeding in Business*, *Nothing but the Tooth: 11 Questions You Should Ask Your Dentist*, *The Habit Formula: Life's Success Equation*, *The Habit Formula: A Parent's Success Equation Kid's Edition*, *The Backward Rule: The Ultimate Way to Hit Any Target*, *The 9 Truths: Don't F*uck Up Your Life*, and *Lipstick Philosophy: Daily Wisdom for the Modern Woman*.

Coming from humble beginnings in a small town in Ohio, Dr. Aldrich continues to strive for success for not only herself and her companies, but for others as well. Knowing that anything is possible drives her creativity to handle issues that plague individuals as well as communities. When you start with children and form good habitual behaviors from the start, you will benefit the community overall when those children grow up and start to serve others.

Dr. Aldrich lives in Copley, Ohio with her husband Steven and their wonderful son, Noah.